Science Fiction, Science Fact!
Ages 5–7

Science Fiction, Science Fact! Ages 5–7 is a book for story-loving primary teachers who want to find a creative way to teach science. Contextualising science in a story that pupils know and love, the book contains a wide range of activities and investigations to help Key Stage 1 pupils engage in science learning, while also extending aspects of the English national curriculum.

The book offers valuable support to busy teachers and, by ensuring science lessons are enjoyable and accessible for pupils, helps children get involved in investigations in a way that is memorable for them. Using coloured illustrations and diagrams throughout, the book contains:

- the relevant scientific context alongside a link to one of eight exciting children's stories;
- clever and unique suggestions to 'storify the science';
- instructions for teachers to give to their pupils;
- tips on how to deliver the lesson in an immersive way;
- guidance on assessing pupils' level of understanding.

Science Fiction, Science Fact! Ages 5–7 is packed full of ideas for weaving science into cross-curricular lessons, and is an invigorating and essential resource for Key Stage 1 teachers and science co-ordinators seeking to inject some creativity into their science lessons.

Jules Pottle is a primary science specialist teacher with experience teaching in primary schools for over twenty years, and a trainer for Storytelling Schools, UK. She won the Primary Science Teaching Trust's Primary Science Teacher of the Year in 2015.

Science Fiction, Science Fact! Ages 5–7

Learning Science through Well-Loved Stories

Jules Pottle

Routledge
Taylor & Francis Group

LONDON AND NEW YORK

First published 2018
by Routledge
2 Park Square, Milton Park, Abingdon, Oxon OX14 4RN

and by Routledge
711 Third Avenue, New York, NY 10017

Routledge is an imprint of the Taylor & Francis Group, an informa business

© 2018 Jules Pottle

British Library Cataloguing-in-Publication Data
A catalogue record for this book is available from the British Library

Library of Congress Cataloging-in-Publication Data
A catalog record has been requested for this book

ISBN: 978-1-138-29095-2 (hbk)
ISBN: 978-1-138-29096-9 (pbk)
ISBN: 978-1-315-26575-9 (ebk)

Typeset in Helvetica
By Florence Production Limited, Stoodleigh, Devon, UK

Printed and bound by CPI Group (UK) Ltd, Croydon, CR0 4YY

For my lovely mum who was always on the sidelines, cheering. And my dad, whose enthusiasm for science built the foundations of this book.

Contents

Acknowledgements

With love and gratitude to my very patient family who supported me while I was writing.

Thanks to Alex Sinclair for his hours of editing and excellent advice on all things scientific.

Thanks also to Sarah Bearchell (*Sarah's Adventure in Science*) for her ideas and enthusiasm.

My thanks also go to Chris Smith of Storytelling Schools, for teaching me to be a storyteller and for his ongoing support. I have included some of Storytelling Schools' methods in this book and I would like to thank Chris for his kind permission in letting me use them here.

And finally, thanks to Rufus Cooper for his amazing illustrations, which have brought this book to life.

Introduction

Why do you need this book?

Science is a crucial part of every child's education.

It engages children in thinking about how things work, it encourages them to be observant and notice patterns, it teaches them to be curious and prompts them to ask pertinent questions that can be tested. We need these skills to be creative, to visualise and, ultimately, to persevere in problem solving.

And yet, primary science is often a second-class citizen. It rarely takes centre stage in the primary classroom as the 'real business of the day'. English and maths dominate the timetable. For many primary teachers, for many reasons, science is a hard subject to tackle.

But everybody loves a good story.

What if you could put a story at the centre of your teaching and have the science and the English tumble out of it?

This book is written for story lovers and for those who find science a little bewildering or dry. It takes the wonder of a good story and helps you to use that story world as a context for science teaching.

I have tried to provide everything you'll need to know about the science as well as the practicalities of setting up the lesson, linking it to the book. There are also ways to record the learning so that you can pick up the book, grab the equipment and run with it!

Why use stories?

Stories create a context for the science. We use science all the time in the real world. To drive a car we need sufficient friction in the tread in our tyres and sufficient thrust from the engine. When you teach science in context, it makes more sense. It stops being an abstract concept (of friction or thrust) and becomes something the children can visualise (the grip on the road or the acceleration of the car).

It helps to put the science into the context of a real world but it could also be a fictional world. What is important is that the world is clear in the mind of the child. In a story, there are also characters with problems to solve. The science is important to the characters so, if we are engaged with the emotions of the characters, then the science becomes important to us.

There are lots of benefits to using stories in education and many studies show that context-based science teaching can be very successful. My experience has shown that it engages children who love science anyway (the non-fiction readers and the factual answer seekers) and it engages the story lovers (the huge novel readers who can suspend reality and live in an entirely fictional world). It seems to cover all the bases.

I once had a child in my class who loved science but wasn't keen on English. During creative writing sessions, his head would be on the desk and the paper would be blank. But during science lessons he was wide awake and thinking, joining in discussions and asking interesting questions. He would only write two lines of story in his English book but he'd write two pages of witty and entertaining story in his science book. Using stories can hook the story lovers into science but it can also hook the science lovers into stories.

How do we use the book?

First, I suggest you read the next chapter, as it will help you set out a lesson that is playful and engaging. There are tips in that chapter that will help you in all your science teaching.

The next eight chapters cover eight picture books. Each story is used to teach a science topic. The last book, *Pirates Love Underpants* is a skills-based topic.

The books and topics included in this book are as shown on the facing page.

Of course, there are lots of books that lend themselves to the teaching of science. I hope you will go out and find more. I chose these ones as they offered links to complete topics rather than bits and pieces from all over the curriculum and because I love these stories.

So, choose a book or choose the science topic and turn to the relevant chapter. I suggest you read the whole chapter before you start teaching and check that you have the equipment you need. You may want to use all the lessons or you may want to dip into them. Use the book as you see fit.

You may want to teach extra lessons alongside the ones in this book, to supplement the children's learning. You may want to explain everything in the science sections to them or just give them what they are ready to digest and understand. You know your class. You'll know when they've understood the science.

You may be working from a different curriculum and only some of the lessons fit your needs. Take the ones that work and invent your own to fit the rest.

I hope it inspires you to get the next generation excited about science.

Picture Book	Storyline	Science concepts
Dinosaur Roar **By Paul Stickland and Henrietta Stickland**	A rhyme about the different features of dinosaurs.	Animals: • Carnivores • Herbivores and omnivores • Parts of the body • Senses
Peace at Last **By Jill Murphy**	Daddy Bear can't get to sleep because the house is too noisy.	Body parts, senses and materials: • Ears • Materials that reduce/amplify sound • Identifying sounds • Choosing materials that are fit for purpose
Traction Man Is Here **By Mini Grey**	Traction Man has all the best outfits. He has an outfit fit for every purpose. Then Granny knits him one that he wasn't expecting.	Properties of materials: • Floating and sinking • Strength • Padding • Insulation
The Storm Whale in Winter **By Benji Davies**	It is winter and Noi's island is covered with snow. He is worried about his friend the whale. Little does he know that his friend will come to his rescue.	Changing materials: • Making ice • Melting ice • Freezing other liquids
The Tiny Seed **By Eric Carle**	The tiny seed blows far away from the mother plant and must land in just the right soil and have just the right conditions to grow into a flower.	Growing plants: • Sorting seeds • Wind dispersal • Planting in different places • Germination • Transporting water • Leaf identification • Bee pollination
Goldilocks and the Three Bears **Traditional**	Goldilocks gets hungry and eats up Baby Bear's porridge. Then, in a new innovation of the story, she eats up Baby Bear's healthy lunch.	Humans: • Babies grow into adults like their parents • What we need to do to survive • Healthy diet • Exercise
The Odd Egg **By Emily Gravett**	Everyone else is hatching eggs but Duck doesn't have one of his own. He adopts a rather large egg and cares for it but what is inside?	Animal life cycles: • Eggs • Incubation • Hatching • Naming local birds and feeding them
Pirates Love Underpants **By Claire Freedman and Ben Cort**	These pirates love their underpants. When they find that another crew of pirates have made off with the treasure, they use their knowledge of knicker elastic to recapture it.	Science skills: • Sorting and grouping • Spotting patterns • Answering a question in different ways • Observing and identifying • Simple tests • Gathering data and recording

1 How to teach a great science lesson

Science lessons should be a real highlight in your week: a chance to be playful and have some fun, a chance to let the children lead their own learning and an opportunity to inject a little awe and wonder. This book gives you all the knowhow you'll need to plan a really exciting lesson, set in the context of a story. In this book, I refer to a range of different types of lesson structures – activities and investigations.

- Activities: the children do or make something in order to 'feel the science' for themselves. Nothing is measured and no data is collected.
- Investigations: the children carry out some kind of test, make measurements and some kind of data is collected or items are sorted as a result of the testing.

In this chapter, I will share with you some of the tricks of the trade that I have learned through twenty-odd years of teaching primary science. They can be summarised as:

- You don't have to know everything
- Be playful
- Talk about it so you can think about it
- Write about it in a focussed and creative way
- Let the children discover it for themselves
- Feel the science
- Put the science in context.

You may find it useful to read this chapter first.

You don't have to know everything

Most primary school teachers have a degree in humanities or arts. Very few have a science degree or even science A levels so it is very common for primary teachers to feel daunted by the thought of teaching science. You are not alone! We have all experienced the hand going up and the question that we just can't answer. I have two stock replies in those circumstances:

- Great question! I have no idea – I'll find out.
- I think this is what happens but I'll check and get back to you.

They both involve a quick conversation with 'Professor Google' (who knows pretty much everything) after the lesson and then a quick return to the question at the start of the next lesson. Remember that your job is to encourage the children to be curious so embrace their questions and be content to discover the answers together. Even great scientists would be keen to tell us that they don't know all the answers!

The point of a primary science lesson is to promote scientific thinking. Very few children will remember every fact that they learned in primary science lessons but they will remember the lesson where they made pop rockets and worked out how to make them go really high. They will remember being allowed to plant their bean seeds in purple paint just to see whether they grew purple plants. Hopefully, they will leave primary school thinking science is fun and knowing how to set up an experiment to test out a question, to satisfy their own curiosity. So, you don't need to be the person who knows everything. You just need to be the person who is willing to help the children find their own answers.

Be playful

Being playful in science lessons is crucial. It is what engages the children. If you give off an air of wonder and excitement about finding out what happens, you'll find it's contagious. It is particularly important with younger children.

The best lessons are the ones where the children are excited about the science. Yes, they'll get overexcited sometimes and yes, it might be both messy and noisy. But a lesson where all the children are making a mess and making a noise, while completely engaged in the task, and being delighted by their own results, is the epitome of good science teaching.

Be prepared to try out their ideas – they'll love you for it. I once set the children a problem as part of a 'separating materials topic'. I mixed rice, steel paper clips and marbles into a tub of water and challenged them to separate out all the elements. I was expecting them to suggest sieves or magnets as a method of separating the items but children are full of surprises. One child suggested that if you launched the tub upwards a few feet, the items would leap upwards out of the water and the water would remain in the tub. I could see this wouldn't work. The other children in the class could see this wouldn't work! But the child who suggested it clearly had a misconception that he needed to test out. So, I let him. We took the tub outside and had a go. It was a fairly controlled launch but it was still a pretty wet experience and the items all stayed mixed in the water! But it was safe, the children remembered it, the misconception was dealt with . . . and we all had fun. I could have simply told him that it wouldn't work but he wouldn't have believed it, without testing it. This is why it is important to have a playful attitude as the teacher.

Sometimes, being playful means being prepared to put on a bit of a show for the children: making the rocket go really high (without showing them how you did it) or pretending you're surprised when your specially weighted cake tin rolls uphill instead of down.

Play can also be the process of fiddling about with something to see what happens or to see how it works. Great scientists, such as Watson and Crick, who discovered the double helix shape of the molecule DNA (and thus revealed the process by which DNA is replicated), refer to the process they used as 'play':

In *The Double Helix* Watson wrote 'All we had to do was to construct a set of molecular models and begin to play' (Watson, 1968). Some people refer to this process as tinkering. Whatever you call it, we need more of it in the primary classroom.

So, encourage playfulness in your classroom and watch the curiosity, creativity and engagement grow.

Talk about it so you can think about it

Science talk is really important. If you give the children time to express their thoughts about what is happening (or what might happen) then you give them time to frame their ideas in their own minds. Talking to another child can also help raise differences in their understanding, which can then be debated and misconceptions can be tackled.

In this book, I give you ways to lead the children to their own answers through discussion. Try not to give them the answer at the start. If you tell them the science, they hear it but they may not process it. In my experience, as it is not their own discovery, they are less likely to engage with it. If you ask them to explain their own idea and they find out they were right – then they have a sense of achievement and delight in the science. In the same way, if they voice a misconception and then find out that the science works in a way they hadn't anticipated, then they are more likely to relearn the science without the misconception. Talking about what might happen helps them to engage with the science so learning can take place.

Science talk needs to leave room for lots of ideas, even if the ideas are not correct. It is all too easy to close down a discussion with the right answer and end the discussion. This stops learning in its tracks. Imagine this situation: a teacher hears a child ask an interesting question – 'Will that puddle freeze if I put an ice cube into it?'

The teacher knows the answer. By answering 'No' she ends the discussion and the child won't have a chance to explore his idea so she chooses to say something else – 'Shall we try it and find out?' Now, there is some engagement with the science. Ice cubes are gathered and the child can put one in the puddle. He discovers that the puddle doesn't freeze. The teacher could leave it there. But if she acts a little surprised and seems curious then she could show the child how to ask further questions such as 'Do we need more ice?' or 'What happens to the ice when you put it in the puddle?' and thus the engagement with the science can be prolonged and developed until the child is able to have some first-hand experience and is able to answer his own question for himself.

Scientific thinking can be shut down in a classroom where the teacher asks the children what they think is happening and stops asking for responses at the first right answer. Once the right answer is confirmed as the right answer, the thinking stops.

So, wherever you are able, keep the talk going, maintain that debate and let the children vocalise their ideas, whether they be right or wrong. Then, let them experience the science and discuss it again. And only, when all the children have engaged with the discussion, lead them through the correct scientific explanation – using the words of the children and the correct scientific vocabulary, side by side.

If you need to get more out of the children without giving away what is right or wrong, you can always say 'Tell me more'.

I was recently involved in a really interesting piece of research that has resulted in some excellent teacher training. Helen Wilson of Oxford Brookes University and Bridget Holligan of Science Oxford decided to test out the idea that stretching the children's minds in science lessons with 'Big Questions' and discussion could have a positive impact on their ability to problem solve in other subjects. They set up the Thinking, Doing, Talking Science Project based on the following idea:

Professor Philip Adey has made the important point that "What the research shows consistently is that if you face children with intellectual challenges and then help them talk through the problems towards a solution, then you almost literally stretch their minds. They become cleverer, not only in the particular topic, but across the curriculum." It can therefore be argued that teachers cannot afford to allow their pupils to miss out on the opportunities for deep thinking.

One method of ensuring this is to incorporate a "Bright Ideas" slot into lessons and this need not take more than ten minutes per session. Science is surely all about thinking and the enjoyment of thinking deeply. Discussing big ideas is more important than finding the right answer and it will obviously be important to establish a classroom atmosphere in which all ideas and responses will be valued.

(Coates and Wilson, 2003)

So, I would encourage you to include games that encourage talk into your science lessons. They often show you what the children already know, highlight misconceptions and provide a safe platform for them to practise making suggestions, thinking out loud, debating or putting forward ideas, in front of their peers.

Write about it in a focussed and creative way

Every school has their own policy on what should be recorded in a science lesson.

For younger children, schools are unlikely to require vast amounts of written reporting on science work. It is more important that the practical work is followed up with discussion and that the child is given an opportunity to tell you about it than it is to put something in a book. For this reason, many of the recording ideas are not written tasks. Instead, they encourage ways to use the learning and ways to show you as the teacher what they have understood.

For older children, with fluent writing skills, you may want to record more. In fact, some schools require all science to be recorded in a full write-up after every session. That might include:

- Question: Which ice-lolly lasts the longest in the hot sun?
- Equipment: Draw the equipment you used and label it.
- Method: Explain how you set up the equipment and how you took the measurements.
- Prediction: Which ice-lolly you think will melt first and why?
- Results: Table of results (time and length) and maybe a bar chart.
- Conclusion: Name the lolly that lasts the longest and explain why.
- Evaluation: How could I improve upon my test design?

This is a long laborious process and is likely to take longer than the practical work.

While I agree that children need to know how to write each section of a full science report, I don't think they need to write every part, every week.

Consider the amount of time that you are allotted to teach science every week. At least half of it should be practical work. Some of it will be needed for settling the children, introducing the topic and engaging the children in the science they are about to do. So, that doesn't leave hours at the end of the lesson for writing about it. So, what do we do?

- Use maths lessons
- Use English lessons
- And use the science lessons!

First, if you plan well in advance, you can use maths lessons to record the data and convert measurements from one unit to another, etc. Embed your maths lesson within the science lesson and use the science data to teach the maths.

Likewise, you can use English lessons to write about what you have learned and I give lots of examples about how to do that in this book. After each lesson described, you'll find suggestions on how to record the children's learning in text types that you may be studying already such as 'play-scripts' or 'explanations'. If you are using the story as the centre of your cross-curricular planning then why not make your recording of the science cross-curricular too?

But what should we record in the science lessons themselves? If the children are already able to write, then write about what you found out (an explanation of what happened with reference to the science) but it need only be a sentence long. In addition, you could choose one of the parts of a full write-up to do after each lesson (e.g. a prediction). Make sure you choose each one at least once per topic and aim to let the children do this unaided on a regular basis, so you can assess what they are able to do. You could:

- focus on predictions (write them before you start the practical work) and, at the end, say if you were correct;
- focus on writing instructions and write a clear method with diagrams of the equipment;
- focus on collecting data – draw up your own table and graph the data;
- focus on conclusions and write a detailed, scientific explanation of what happened, including diagrams;
- focus on the design of your experiment. Draw the equipment you used and annotate it. At the end of the session, evaluate the design of your experiment;
- write a full report, including all the elements.

Of course, you may need a quick drawing, a photo or a clear title on the page so the children remember what they have done in each lesson but writing a whole report every time turns the science lesson into an English lesson and valuable science learning time is lost.

If your children are not yet able to write, give them a chance to explain orally so they can frame their ideas in their own words.

Let the children discover it for themselves

If you present a child with some science in an authoritative 'this is how it works' voice, you are showing them **your** science. It is not **their** science. They may be interested or they may not be However, if you let the children discover the science, then they own it. They own it in the same way that they own that den that they built at lunchtime!

So, when you start something new with the children, give them time to explore. Give them time to play. If you are investigating forces, spend time playing with cars and ramps, getting some experience of what happens. They may never have played with equipment like this before. Then, when they have built speed bumps to slow the cars down and tried really steep slopes to make them go further, then, they'll have their own ideas about what question they would like to investigate in a fair test. They'll be investigating their own idea – they'll own it.

It might take a while but this time is not wasted. Many great scientists discovered a great many things that didn't work before they discovered the one that did!

So, make time for play in the primary classroom. Give the children time to handle equipment before they have to use it to collect data. Let them see what happens so that they can come up with their own ideas that they are motivated to test out. Let them discover science for themselves. Yes, this may take a little longer but, as Johnston (2004) explains in the following article, the time spent on letting children discover the science for themselves pays dividends in terms of engagement in the science.

> It seems that in busy primary classrooms the opportunities to observe and to develop observation skills can easily be overlooked, but finding time for children to observe phenomena and to follow their own interests will pay dividends in supporting quality outcomes in all areas of scientific enquiry and understandings. In a discovery approach, the outcomes will be greater in terms of all enquiry skills, as well as understandings and attitudes, where the children:
>
> - are central to the learning;
> - explore and discover things about the world around them that arise from their own initial curiosity and observations;
> - construct their own understandings through their observation and exploration;
> - are supported by teachers and peers through social interaction.
>
> (Johnston, 2004, pp. 21–3)

Feel the science

Science lessons should be as practical as your space and equipment will allow. Wherever possible (and safe), give the children a chance to return to the practical science activities to explore any further ideas they may have.

Children are much more likely to retain information if they have seen it happen or felt it with their own hands. And children are more likely to explore the science if they have free access to science equipment in the their classroom and outdoor areas.

Misconceptions often happen because the children haven't experienced the science at first hand. Imagine giving a class some objects and asking them to test whether they will float or sink. A common misconception is that heavy things sink and light ones float. If you include some surprising objects in the selection you can get the children to test out their misconceptions and come to a better understanding. Surprising objects might be: pumice stone which floats (stones normally sink), different plastics (some float and some sink), aluminium block and aluminium take-away-container/drinks can (only the one with air inside will float). In an activity like this, you'll find the surprising ones are the ones that get all the attention and generate a lot of talk.

Practical science lessons do require equipment and primary schools often work on a tight budget and don't have large sets of science equipment. But you can do a lot of science with household objects so you'll find you can do many of the experiments suggested in this book without specialist equipment.

With a rowdy class, prone to messing about with equipment, I have found the trick is to move fast. Stop the process when one or two groups have gathered some useable data. Give a few warnings before you stop so that everyone knows to speed up. But stop before there are children with time on their hands to think about ways to mess about with the equipment!

You can also have an extra extension task to hand to occupy the very speedy group – there's always one.

Put the science into context

Children understand the science most clearly, when they can see the practical application of the science: floating and sinking is clearly understood when you start building rafts to get off the desert island. This is what has led me to the teaching of science through stories. Once the child has engaged with the characters in the story and lived alongside them as you read the book, they care far more about whether that raft will float and carry the character home. It is unlikely, in our everyday lives, that we will need to solve a life or death problem by building a raft, so building a raft for a character (who is real in the imagination) is the next best thing. Providing a context in which the science is useful is a way to engage the children and this could be a story based context.

This context needs to be real in the mind of the child but it doesn't have to be true! It could be fictional. Of course, fantasy stories where magic changes the way that the fantasy world operates might be muddling if used in this context but there are many fictional stories based in our world with science that operates in the same way as in the real world. Alternatively, there are also fantasy elements that can be challenged and tested to see whether they could work in the real world, such as working out whether gobstoppers really can be everlasting. So, with a little careful treatment, many stories can provide a context for science investigations and they work well together.

As Pie Corbett beautifully put it, 'Without science we are lost. Without story we are trapped alone in the darkness of ourselves. For too long, these companions have wandered on separate tracks' (Smith and Pottle, 2015, p. ix).

The rest of this book is dedicated to the nuts and bolts of bringing science alive to children by engaging them with science in the context of a fictional world.

––––––––––––––––––––––––

2 *Dinosaur Roar*

Paul Stickland and Henrietta Stickland
(2014)

TOPIC PLANNER

Story link	Science: Carnivores, herbivores and senses	Activity	Page
What is a carnivore?	Carnivores and herbivores	Carnivore chase game (activity)	9
Sorting carnivores and herbivores	Mini-beasts can be carnivores too! Identifying and sorting mini-beasts	Naming and sorting mini-beasts (activity)	12
Carnivore clues	Features of predator and prey Comparing Designing for a purpose	Features of dinosaurs and herbivores Design-a-saurus! (activity)	16–17
Just like a dinosaur	The vertebrate form Senses Observing and comparing	What's the same and what's different? Sensing the world like a dinosaur (activity)	20–1

WHAT IS A CARNIVORE?

Story link

The small green dinosaur on the first page thinks he is about to be eaten.

THE SCIENCE: Carnivore and herbivores

The word carnivore is made from words meaning meat eater and herbivore from the words meaning plant eater. Meat in this sense means any other animal, not just the kind of meat that the children may be familiar with, such as cows or fish. It can mean insects.

Plants are made of very long structures of carbohydrates. These molecules are really hard to digest and break down into useful building blocks for animal tissue growth. Digesting plant matter requires a very long gut, to allow time for digestion to happen as the food passes through. It also requires the help of particular bacteria. In order to get sufficient nutrition from their food, plant eaters (herbivores) must spend a large proportion of their life eating and chewing.

It is much more efficient to eat meat. Meat is made from protein and easily digested into its constituent amino acids, which can be used for making new animal tissue, allowing the meat eater to grow. Meat is packed full of calories (energy) whereas plant food has far fewer calories. Consequently, carnivores spend a lot less of their life eating than herbivores. The downside is that their food may not want to be eaten and may take a bit of tracking down. Grass doesn't run away but a zebra does!

What do the children need to know?

*   Carnivore means meat eater and herbivore means plant eater.
*   Some dinosaurs ate meat but others ate plants.

ACTIVITY: Carnivore chase game

You will need:

*   bean bags (green if you have them)
*   a large space to play.

Storify the science

Read the whole book through once, at a good speed so you can enjoy the rhythm and the rhyme of it. Return to the first page and look closely at the picture. Ask the children what the little dinosaur is thinking. It is clear that he is alarmed and maybe he thinks he is going to be eaten. Ask the children what the little green dinosaur is eating. Ask whether the little green dinosaur would eat the T-Rex. Elicit the idea that T-Rex eats small dinosaurs and introduce the term carnivore and explain that it means meat-eater.

Draw a plant on the board. Ask the children what made the plant grow. Talk about growing plants. They may know that a plant needs sunshine and rain. Tell them that the plant uses water, air and sunlight to make its own food so it can grow. Plants don't have to eat.

Animals can't make their own food so they must eat.

 Set the challenge

You are going to play a game to show how carnivores get their food.

- You need to be in groups of six and you'll need room to run around.
- Pretend the beanbags are plants. Place the plants over the floor/ground.
- Choose five children to be herbivores and one to be a carnivore. The herbivores will get a few seconds' head start. They can go after the first countdown. The carnivore has to wait for the second count down.
- Count down like this:

    Herbivores eat plants that grow,

    3, 2, 1, GO!
- Now the herbivores can start to 'eat up' (pick up) as many plants (beanbags) as they can.
- Count down again:

    Carnivores crunch meat and bones

    3, 2, 1, GO!
- The carnivore now has ten seconds to catch a herbivore. They can't eat plants so they must catch a herbivore for their dinner.

If they catch (tag) a herbivore, they win the plants (beanbags) that the herbivore had gathered because the nutrients in the plants would end up in the body of the herbivore and then get eaten by the carnivore. Keep these plants in a pile at the side of the room/space. The herbivore who has been caught is 'out' and must sit down at the side for the remainder of the game.

The game restarts (put all the other plants back on the floor) and do both countdowns again. Now there are only four herbivores to chase.

Again, keep any plants that are won by catching herbivores in the pile.

Play a third round and count up the plants won by the carnivore. This is your carnivore score.

Swap roles and begin the game again with a new carnivore. See if you can beat the first carnivore score!

Remember, the carnivore can't eat plants so you can only win them by catching herbivores.

Teacher's top tips

The important learning point here is the fact that the carnivore's food is a herbivore but the herbivore got their food from plants. The plant grows, the herbivore eats it and passes the energy on to the carnivore.

You want to avoid having too many players in the space as children picking up beanbags may bump heads if they are closely packed. Better to play with a few and have the rest chanting the countdowns from the side. Then play again with another group.

You may want to keep a herbivore score so that children playing the part of herbivores stay motivated too. They'll need to be old enough to count up their own beanbags over three rounds.

KEY QUESTIONS to help children to move towards an understanding:

- What did the herbivores do to stay alive?
- What did the carnivores do to stay alive?

 # What next?

If you want to record your findings in a creative way then you could:

- Ages 4–5: create a small world for dinosaurs in the sand tray or garden. Role-play herbivores eating the vegetation while the carnivore hunts them.
- Write a poem entitled 'Going on a herbivore hunt'. Describe all the places you visit as you chase the herbivores.
- Make up a board game. The herbivore starts ten spaces ahead of the carnivore. Roll a dice to move. The carnivore must catch up the herbivore to win the game. The herbivore must keep ahead of the carnivore to win.

 # Look out for evidence of scientific thinking and learning

- The children make observations, e.g. in the picture, the T-Rex has big teeth to eat up the herbivore.
- The children make links, e.g. all the beanbags ended up with the carnivore. (The herbivore eats the plants and then the carnivore eats the herbivore so the energy from the plants ends up with the carnivore in the end.)

———————————

SORTING CARNIVORES AND HERBIVORES

Story link

The dinosaurs are all eating different things for their lunch.

THE SCIENCE: Mini-beasts can be carnivores too!

There is no 'rule of thumb' to instantly tell just by looking at an animal whether it is a herbivore or a carnivore. However, once they open their mouths you'll see that their teeth/mouthparts (and digestive system) are adapted to the food they eat.

Some animals are omnivores. 'Omni' means everything. The animals eat both meat and plant matter. Once the children begin to sort the animals they will realise that they need this third group.

N.B. In the picture referred to below, there is a flying dinosaur with feathers. There is a theory that there may have been flying dinosaurs and these may have had feathers. These could be the ancestors of the birds that we have on Earth today.

What do the children need to know?

*   The term carnivore and herbivore can be applied to animals other than dinosaurs.
*   Animals that eat meat and plant matter are called omnivores.

ACTIVITY: Naming and sorting mini-beasts (and other animals)

You will need:

*   nets
*   pots
*   clean paintbrushes
*   large white sheet
*   trays/tanks in which to view animals
*   magnifying glasses
*   identification sheets
*   pictures or models of large familiar reptiles and mammals, e.g. crocodile, elephant, horse
*   enlarged pictures of familiar mini-beasts, e.g. ladybird, spider, caterpillar.

Storify the science

Read the book again, if you like. Turn to the penultimate and the last page. Look closely at the pictures. You could use a visualiser to put the image onto the whiteboard. The dinosaurs are all eating different foods. Some are going after the flying dinosaur, others are eating leaves or berries.

Ask the children what they notice about the two dinosaurs who have their eyes fixed on the flying dinosaur. Elicit that they have big, scary-looking teeth. The teeth of the herbivores are not visible in the pictures. Ask the children if the herbivores have teeth. Give them time to talk about this with a partner.

Some look like they have beaks. Some may have teeth inside. None of them need the enormous dagger-like fangs of the T-Rex.

Ask the children if all carnivores have teeth like T-Rex. Look at the picture of the horse. Ask the children what it eats and look for fangs. (It eats grass so no fangs.)

Look at the crocodile. (It eats animals so it has fangs.)

Look at the elephant. Note the tusks. Ask the children what they think the tusks are. Elicit that elephant teeth are further back inside the mouth. (It eats grass so no fangs.) The tusks are used for defence, digging, lifting and gathering food.

Now look at the mini-beasts. Do any of them have fangs? Discuss that some carnivores have different mouth parts.

 Set the challenge

You are going to find some mini-beasts and identify them. Then you can find out what they eat. Find out which mini-beasts are carnivores and which are herbivores.

There are lots of good ways to collect mini-beasts. You could:

- spread a big white sheet under a tree and shake the tree;
- sweep a net back and forth through long grass;
- look closely in the grass, under hedges or under stones to find mini-beasts and use a clean soft paintbrush to brush them into a collecting pot;
- you could leave a piece of wood or card on shady ground for a week and look underneath to find what has moved in!

Once you have looked at them and identified them, take a photo or draw the mini-beast. Then you must put them back where you found them.

Next, use books or a website to help you find out whether the mini-beast is a carnivore or a herbivore.

Sort your mini-beasts into groups according to what they eat.

How many groups did you end up with?

Teacher's top tips

The important skills here are careful observation and identification of the mini-beasts. Use hand lenses to see the details. Encourage children to put the lens close to their eye and lean in close to the mini-beast they are observing.

Ideally, you want to encourage the children to name all the animals and then to find out whether they are carnivores or herbivores. You may need to have this information ready prepared on the identification sheet, if your children are very young, so you can do the sorting activity together.

You may find you have mini-beasts that eat both meat and plants. At this point, introduce the term **omnivore**.

KEY QUESTIONS to help children to move towards an understanding:

- What can you see?
- Look again, what else can you see?
- Does it look the same as . . .?
- Have you seen one of these before? Where?

- What do you know about it?
- Which part does it use for eating?
- Can you match it to the picture? What is it called?
- Which mini-beasts go in the same group?

 # What next?

If you want to record your findings in a creative way then you could:

- Ages 4–5: take a photo of each mini-beast you found and stick the pictures into groups of carnivores and herbivores.
- Make a set of 'Top Trumps' style card. The categories might be length, number of legs, number of sections in body (spider – 2, insect – 3, earthworm – lots). Of course carnivores will trump herbivores! Make sure you include some tiny mini-beasts and enormous dinosaurs.
- Role-play being different mini-beasts or dinosaurs at dinner time. Who will be having meat and who will be eating plants? You could even have a carnivore and herbivore picnic with lots of meat and vegetables to try.
- Make a mini book of carnivores and herbivores. On each page draw a different dinosaur or mini-beast and say whether it is a carnivore or herbivore or an omnivore.

 # Look out for evidence of scientific thinking and learning

- The children use hand lenses to closely observe the mini-beasts.
- The children make observations, e.g. I think they eat with those bits near the front.
- The children make links, e.g. none of the beetles have got teeth.
- The children ask questions, e.g. do all the beetles eat meat? If they eat other insects does that count as meat?
- The children can sort the mini-beasts according to what they eat.

CARNIVORE CLUES

Story link

The dinosaurs have different features according to whether they are predator or prey.

THE SCIENCE: Features of predator and prey

These are general principles but as always there are lots of exceptions!

Predators (carnivores) need to be able to see in front of them in order to hunt so their eyes are often positioned at the front and many larger predatory animals have binocular vision, like humans, that allows them to accurately judge distance and pounce on their prey.

Prey (herbivores and some carnivores) need to be able to see what is coming to get them so they need good all round vision. Their eyes are often positioned at the sides.

Invertebrate predators and prey (such as the mini-beasts you found in the last session) may use vibrations to detect movement rather than using the sense of sight. Some won't actively hunt but lie in wait for their prey or trap them, such as a spider.

Predators (carnivores) will have teeth, beaks, claws or mouthparts that are sharp and curved for catching and tearing their prey.

Herbivores will tend to have flattened back teeth or mouth parts that can grind in order to grind up the plant material.

Predators may be camouflaged so that they blend in with their surroundings and can creep up on their prey.

Prey may be camouflaged so that they are harder for the predators to find. Sometimes they have markings that look scary to predators and sometimes they have markings that confuse the predators when they are running.

Some animals will be predators and are also eaten by other predators so they are both predator and prey.

What do the children need to know?

• The bodies of animals are adapted to fit the lives they lead.

 ACTIVITY: Design-a-saurus!

You will need:

- a trip to a natural history museum with dinosaur skeletons
- OR plastic dinosaur models (scientifically accurate) or large pictures of dinosaurs to look at that are drawn to look realistic, not cartoon-like
- pictures of dinosaur skulls with teeth
- a fossil
- pictures of crocodiles and lizards (some coloured to match their habitat)
- boxes and recycled pots for junk modelling
- glue and tape
- paint.

 Storify the science

Turn to the page where it mentions spiky and lumpy dinosaurs. Look at the spines and the spikes and lumps. Ask the children what they think those spikes and lumps are for. Give them time to talk to a partner about this and listen to all their many answers. Elicit that they could be for defence against predators.

Ideally, the next part of the session would be held in a museum full of dinosaur skeletons but if real skeletons are unavailable, use the pictures and models as described below.

Look at the realistic models/pictures of dinosaurs (as opposed to the drawings in the story book that are modified to look happy, etc.) and look for spikes, spines and other protective features. Find out whether these dinosaurs were eaten by other dinosaurs. See if they needed these spikes and lumps for protection.

Look closely at the dinosaur skull pictures and spot the differences between the types of teeth – sharp and pointy for carnivorous predators, e.g. T-Rex but flatter and wider in the herbivores, e.g. Iguanadon. (Flat teeth indicate grinding. Some herbivores had sharper teeth but didn't grind their food.)

Look at the colours of the dinosaurs in the story book and compare them to the more realistic pictures of dinosaurs. Are they the same? Ask the children which they think is right – the bright colours in the story or the muter, greener colour of the dinosaur models/pictures in non-fiction books.

Show the children the fossil. Explain that dinosaurs are extinct. The only remains we have are fossils, like this. Does the fossil show us the colour? Elicit that we don't know what colour the dinosaurs were so scientists have guessed by looking at the reptiles that are still alive today – such as crocodiles and lizards. (N.B. There is new evidence being found all the time.)

Show the children some photos of crocodiles and lizards. Note that lizards that live in the sandy desert are sand coloured while those that live in trees are green. Discuss how this camouflage helps to hide them from predators. Dinosaurs were probably coloured to give them camouflage.

Set the challenge

You are going to design your own dinosaur. Decide whether your dinosaur will be a carnivore or a herbivore. When you design your dinosaur, think about:

- whether your dinosaur has to run or reach up high – do they stand on two feet or four?;
- what your dinosaur has to do to gather/catch their food so you can design the legs and claws;
- what kind of teeth your dinosaur has;
- where your dinosaur lives and what colour your dinosaur should be.

Once you've made your dinosaur you can give it a name.

Teacher's top tips

The important skills here are using the knowledge they have gained about different dinosaurs to design their own new species.

Listen out for them making suggestions and choices based on observations, e.g. I need pointy bits of card for the teeth and claws.

Listen out for them making suggestions about the features of the dinosaur based on what it eats or where it lives, e.g. my dinosaur has big feet so it won't sink in the sand.

KEY QUESTIONS to help children to move towards an understanding:

- What do you want to use?
- Why did you choose that?
- What would be the best thing to use for . . .?
- Can you find something the right shape for . . .?

What next?

If you want to record your findings in a creative way then you could:

- Ages 4–5: show your model to an adult and explain why you chose the features on your dinosaur.
- Write a poem about your new dinosaur to echo the poem in the book. Make sure you mention all the features you designed.
- Draw a diagram of your dinosaur and annotate it with all the features you designed and what they are for. Make a class book of everyone's dinosaurs and call it 'The Spotter's Guide to Dinosaurs'.
- Draw a wanted poster for your dinosaur. Describe it clearly. Now imagine what crime your dinosaur committed! You could even tell the story of what your dinosaur got up to.
- Role-play being an explorer going into the prehistoric jungle and finding your dinosaur. Make a video of yourself, dressed as the explorer, finding and describing your model dinosaur.

Look out for evidence of scientific thinking and learning

- The children design their own dinosaur.
- The children make a model of a dinosaur that has features deliberately chosen for a carnivore or herbivore.

JUST LIKE A DINOSAUR

Story link

The dinosaurs are vertebrates just like us.

THE SCIENCE: The vertebrate form

In the animal kingdom, there are two main groups – vertebrates and invertebrates. Vertebrates includes fish, reptiles (including dinosaurs), amphibians, birds and mammals.

All vertebrates have an internal skeleton with a backbone made up of many vertebrae (individual bones in the spine), which allows great flexibility and movement. They also have other similar features such as a skull, ribcage and a similar pattern of bones in any limbs.

The theory of evolution suggests that as all vertebrates have so much in common, it is likely that all vertebrates share a common ancestor and that this ancestor may have been a type of fish.

As humans and dinosaurs are both vertebrates, they have some similarities, although the evidence we have about dinosaurs is mostly limited to bony structures that have been fossilised. Soft tissues, such as skin and internal organs need very specific conditions to be preserved so less evidence of soft tissue parts of dinosaurs has been found.

What do the children need to know?

- Humans and dinosaur skeletons both have a backbone.
- There are lots of parts of vertebrate bodies that are similar and we have the same senses.

ACTIVITY: What's the same and what's different?

You will need:

- a large photocopy of the very long dinosaur
- a picture of a dinosaur skeleton
- a model of a human skeleton or a picture.

For challenge one (requires adult supervision):

- child sized disposable plastic gloves (available on the internet – avoid latex if you have children with latex allergy);
- tray of basil seeds soaked in water;
- tray of kinetic sand (available on the internet, not edible – adult supervision required);
- tray of water beads (available on the internet, not edible – adult supervision required);
- tray of instant snow (available on the internet, not edible – adult supervision required);
- tray of different grades of sandpaper;
- trays of other safe materials with interesting textures.

For challenge two:

- speakers to play music;
- card to roll into cones.

For challenge three:

- opaque plastic pots;
- loose woven fabric (to make lids);
- elastic bands (to hold lids on);
- highly scented foods, e.g. lemon, orange, pineapple, onion;
- foods with little discernible smell, e.g. rice, sugar, pasta.

For the finale:

- a willing adult (young children can't effectively block their noses);
- orange juice, apple juice and cranberry juice;
- clean cups;
- blindfold.

You may want to spread out this section over a few days for younger children or, with older children, you could run it as a carousel of activities.

 ## Storify the science

Look at the very long dinosaur in the book. Have a child stand up next to the big photocopy. You could even have a photo of the child and a large copy of the long dinosaur at the same size, to make the comparison easier. Ask the children to look at the two 'animals' (they'll probably tell you the child is not an animal) and ask them if they can find anything the same on both animals.

Eventually, you should notice that both have two eyes, four limbs and a mouth and nostrils. They both have knees/elbows on each leg. Annotate these to show the similarities.

The dinosaur also has a tail. Look at the dinosaur and human skeletons. They both have a backbone. This continues into the tail in the dinosaur. Look closely at the coccyx of the human and show that there are bones that are the remnant of a tail that humans don't need anymore. Dinosaurs and humans are both vertebrates. We have many of the same bones on the inside. Note the ribcage, skull and pelvis are all recognisable in both.

Look at human hands and dinosaur feet. The dinosaur has claws where we have nails.

Just like lizards, many dinosaurs had scales while our skin is soft. They walked on their feet just like dogs and cats and would have had tough skin on the pads of their feet. Their hands weren't as sensitive as ours. That might make a difference to the way dinosaurs experience the world.

 # Set the challenge

You are going to find out how your hands differ from dinosaur feet.

Our hands are very sensitive and can give us lots of information about the world when we touch things.

- Put a glove on one hand, to act like thick dinosaur skin, and leave the other bare.
- Explore all the different materials with both hands.
- Does it feel the same with both hands?
- What can you feel differently?
- Can you sort the sandpaper into groups according to how it feels? Can you feel it clearly with both hands?

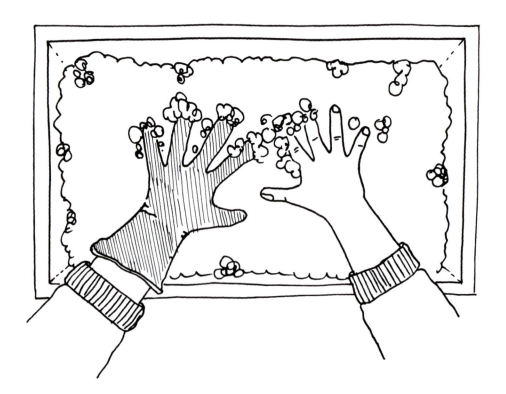

Teacher's top tips

The important skills here are observing using all the senses so allow plenty of time to explore. Talk to the children throughout so that you can help them to observe more thoroughly.

Kinetic sand is very messy – you may want to put a cloth down to protect the carpet and wear aprons!

KEY QUESTIONS to help children to move towards an understanding:

- What do you want to try?
- Why did you choose that?
- Do they all feel like that?
- What words can you think of to describe it?
- Is it like anything else?
- What do you want to try next?

Return to the book

Look again at the picture of the very long dinosaur. The human has outer ears but the long dinosaur does not. Ask the children if they think that the dinosaur can hear. Give them time to talk to a partner about this and listen to all their ideas. Point out that lizards have no outer ear but they have all the parts of the inner ear inside and can hear. So we're pretty sure that dinosaurs could hear too.

 # Set the second challenge – hearing

You are going to find out what our ear flaps do.

- Roll the card into a cone shape.
- Hold the cone shape next to your ear – like this.

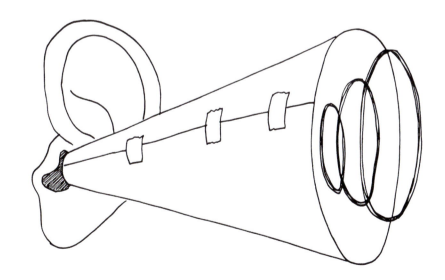

Your teacher will play some music. Listen to the music with the ear cone and listen without. What difference does it make?

Teacher's top tips

The important skills here are observing using all the senses, so allow plenty of time to explore. Talk to the children throughout so that you can help them to observe more thoroughly.

Our outer ear, the pinna, collects the sound but the actual process of sensing the vibrations caused when sounds are made happens in our inner ear, just like the lizard. The cone should make the sound louder, just like our pinna makes the sound louder.

KEY QUESTIONS to help children to move towards an understanding:

- What do you notice?
- What happens if you take it away?
- What do you think is happening?

Return to the book

Look again at the picture of the very long dinosaur. He has two nostrils just above his mouth. Mark the nostrils on the picture of the human. Ask the children what our noses and nostrils are for.

When animals hunt, they use their noses to follow the scent of their food and this helps them find what they are looking for. Dinosaur skeletons show that they had the part of the brain needed to think about smells and they had noses. (Scientists are still working out where the nostrils were exactly as most of our dinosaur knowledge comes from fossilised bones, not the soft fleshy parts.)

 ## Set the third challenge

You are going to see whether you can detect your food using your nose, like a dinosaur.

- Your teacher will give you some pots.
- Using only your nose, try to work out what is in each pot.
- Which foods were easy to detect?
- Which foods were hard to detect?
- Try making some pots of your own. What will you put in them? Why?

 ## Teacher's top tips

The important skills here are observing using all the senses so allow plenty of time to explore. Talk to the children throughout so that you can help them to observe more thoroughly.

KEY QUESTIONS to help children to move towards an understanding:

- What do you want to try?
- Why did you choose that?
- Do they all smell like that?
- What words can you think of to describe it?
- Is it like anything else?
- What do you want to try next?

 Finale

Recap on all the senses we have explored today and note that many familiar animals (particularly mammals) have exactly the same senses.

One of these is taste. Ask the children what we use to taste our food and drink. They will probably indicate mouths or tongues.

- Ask your willing adult helper to come and help you to understand the sense of taste.
- First, blindfold the helper.
- Next, ask them to hold their nose and take a sip from each cup (apple juice, orange juice and cranberry juice). Make a big show of pouring each cup so the children know what is being tasted but the adult doesn't.
- After each sip, ask the adult how it tasted and ask them to guess what they were drinking.

(It should be hard to tell the difference when their nose is blocked.)

- Now repeat the taste test with nose unblocked and ask them to describe each flavour.
- Now they should be able to taste the difference. (Prime them to make a big show of how tart the cranberry juice is.)

Ask the children which parts of their body the adult was using to taste. Discuss that the adult couldn't taste well with her nose blocked so we must be using our noses and our tongues to taste.

 What next?

If you want to record your findings in a creative way then you could:

- Ages 4–5: cut up a picture of a dinosaur skeleton. Can you put it back together the right way? Label the parts you know.
- Make a new book about dinosaurs and humans. On some pages draw things that are the same about humans and dinosaurs and on other pages draw things that are different.
- Imagine being a dinosaur at your school. What would be difficult for you to do? Write a story about the day the dinosaur came to school.
- Draw a big poster for a dinosaur classroom. Label all the parts of the dinosaur's body and say what they are for.

- Role-play being a dinosaur expert. Talk about a picture of a dinosaur or dinosaur skeleton and explain what each part of the body does.

 ## Look out for evidence of scientific thinking and learning

- The children use all their senses to explore the textures, sounds and smells.
- The children make observations, e.g. this feels slimy.
- The children make links, e.g. the gloves stop me touching things so everything feels different in gloves.
- The children ask questions, e.g. is this a stronger smell?
- The children test ideas to find answers, e.g. I think the dinosaur might have very thick skin. Can I try two layers of gloves?
- The children can sort the sandpaper (with their bare hand) into course and fine.

N.B. There's a nice activity in *The Odd Egg* chapter where you hatch bicarbonate of soda eggs. You could put dinosaurs inside to adapt it for this topic. See p. 160.

———————————

3 *Peace at Last*

Jill Murphy (1980)

TOPIC PLANNER

Story link	Science: Sound and hearing	Activity	Page
What a noisy night!	Hearing with our ears Observing and grouping	Identifying ears Finding the ears on humans and other animals (activity)	28–30
Can we make it quieter?	Making noises quieter Choosing the best material	Materials that reduce the sound Selecting the most effective materials to reduce the sound (investigation)	34–5
Watery noises	Some materials make loud noises Testing and grouping	Investigating dripping noises Testing objects and materials to see which ones would keep Mr Bear awake if water dripped on them (investigation)	39
Sounds in the garden at night	Using our ears to identify sounds Listening carefully	Identifying sounds in the garden Recording sounds in the garden and identifying those other have recorded to see which would keep Mr Bear awake (activity)	43
Shhh . . . Let's help Mr Bear sleep!	Making noises quieter Testing and choosing the best material	Making ear defenders Choosing materials to make ear defenders to reduce the volume of Mrs Bear's snoring (investigation)	46

WHAT A NOISY NIGHT

Story link
The noise keeps Mr Bear awake.

THE SCIENCE: Hearing with our ears

Sounds are made when an object vibrates.

The vibrating object knocks into the particles of air around it and these particles knock into the particles next to them. This sets off a wave of sound that travels outwards in all directions from the source of the sound, like a ripple from a stone being dropped in a pond.

Although you might imagine a wave of sound like a wave in the sea, the sound wave is not actually going up and down. Instead, there are areas where the air particles are all squashed up together – they are compressed. The vibrating object pushes upon and compresses the air particles next to it and they in turn compress the air particles next to them. This creates a compression wave.

When the wave reaches our ear drum (at the end of the ear canal) we sense the vibration with a complex set of ear bones, fluid filled tubes and hairs. Our brains perceive this as sound. Different sounds cause different vibrations and these are sensed as different sounds by the structures in our ears. There are some great videos on the internet that show these structures at work if you'd like to see them in action.

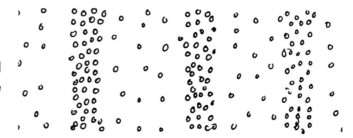

The outer part of our ear is called the pinna. Not all animals have an outer ear. The purpose of the outer ear is to collect sound and funnel it into our ear canal. Animals can often move their outer ears to collect more sound from a particular direction.

ACTIVITY: Identifying ears

You will need:

- lots of animal pictures or models with a variety of ear shapes and positions, e.g. rabbit, sheep, snake, lizard, frog, fish, bird, elephant, dog
- live animals you can bring into the classroom, e.g. woodlouse, worm, ants, beetles and any pets you might have access to, e.g. rabbit, dog, guinea pig, snake, tortoise, etc. (Check your health and safety advice from school and ensure the animals are safe and well cared for in school and returned to their proper environment. You can find great advice on this in the 'Be Safe' booklet from ASE, available from the ASE website.)
- hand lenses for small animals.

Storify the science

Read the whole story to the children. Take time to look at all the pictures and encourage engagement by joining in with Mr Bear every time he exclaims, 'Oh No, I can't stand this!'

Look at Mr Bear in the book, or a teddy, and find his ears. Discuss where they are on his head. Put your hands on your head to be ears and discuss other familiar animals such as rabbits and elephants and discuss where their ears are and what shape they are.

Ask the children what they think ears do. Give them time to talk to a partner about it. In an elephant they help keep the animal cool. On a dog they can show whether the dog is feeling playful or wary. Elicit that the primary function is for hearing.

Ask the children if they can move their ears. Discuss why rabbits can move theirs. (They need to hear predators coming from all directions.)

Ask the children how they know animals can hear. Discuss animal responses to different noises.

Ask the children to experiment by using their hands to block their ears to see if they can still hear one another. Discuss which bit they are blocking to ascertain that it is, in fact, the hole that goes inside that we block to keep the sound out.

Ask children whether they can hear with any other part of their bodies. Some children will be aware that very loud, deep noises, such as rock music, can be felt in our chest.

Ask the children what it might be like to be deaf and how might that feel. Discuss what they would miss. Ask how else could they communicate?

Imagine having really big outer ears like a dog or a rabbit. Ask the children what they think it would be like. Cup hands around ears and listen to each other. They should hear an increase in volume if they pull the pinna (our outer ear) forward a little and use their hands to add to its size.

Set the challenge

You are going to find the ears on these animals and see whether they have big outer ears, small outer ears or just a hole. You might not be able to see the ears on the animal at all.

Draw some of the ears you see.

Look at where the ears are.

Can you sort the animals into groups depending on the ears you can see?

Teacher's top tips

The important skills here are observation and grouping so give the children plenty of time to look and explore.

If you can get larger animals into school, you'll be able to show them the ear canal of a dog, for example, under the outer ear flap.

As insects and other invertebrates do not have obvious outer ears like the dog, the children may assume they have no hearing structures and cannot hear so you may want to discuss this as you meet the animals.

As always, watch out for children with allergies and make sure the animals you bring into the classroom are suitable and safe for this task.

'Pets at Home' and other organisations in your area may offer sessions where they bring animals into school for the day.

There are lots of action songs about ears that you could use to reinforce where ears on animals are located. You could sing 'Heads and shoulders, knees and toes' with a snake or an insect! Or you could sing 'Do your ears hang low?'.

You could also play listening games such as 'Chinese Whispers'.

KEY QUESTIONS to help children to move towards an understanding:

- What do you notice about this animal?
- What can you see with the magnifying glass?
- Are they all like that?
- Can you find ones that are the same in some way?
- Can you describe this one?
- Do these belong together?
- Why?

Little extras

If you play some loud music with a heavy beat, you can feel it pounding in your chest which might help the children to understand what it is like to feel vibrations. You can even put rice on a metal tray and balance it on the bass speaker – you can see the rice jump in time to the beat. Choose a pop song with a strong bass beat for this. You could even relate this to deaf drummers such as Evelyn Glennie and explain that they feel the beat with their bodies.

 # What next?

If you want to record your findings in a creative way then you could:

- Ages 4–5: make a mini book of your animal pictures and label the ears (if they have any) on each one.
- Dress up as a large furry animal with outer ears. Choose or make the right kind of ears and fix them in the right place on your costume. Tell the rest of your class about your ears and how you use them.
- Make a big sorting diagram and stick pictures of animals with different ears into different groups and write labels about the different ears.
- Role-play a conversation between Baby Bear and Mr Bear. Baby Bear wants to know where the ears are on a particular animal. Mr Bear can tell him all about it.

 # Look out for evidence of scientific thinking and learning

- The children use hand lenses to observe the animals.
- The children make observations, e.g. the woodlouse hasn't got any ear flaps.
- The children make links, e.g. the rabbit can catch more sound with his big ears and that's good so he can hear if a fox is coming to eat him.
- The children ask questions, e.g. I can't hear properly under water. Can a dog hear under water? Or 'I wonder if the woodlouse can hear'.
- The children can sort the animals, e.g. big ear flaps, small ear flaps and no ear flaps or ears on the side of your head vs ears on the top.

CAN WE MAKE IT QUIETER?

Story link
The clock is noisy.

 THE SCIENCE: Making noises quieter

To make a sound quieter you can move away from the source of the sound. The sound can only get so far, as the waves of sound will eventually become less intense as they travel further and run out of energy. In fact, this sound energy is eventually transferred to the air molecules as heat. Sound energy becomes heat energy and so the sound reduces as it travels away from the source. But that's too much information for little people!

You can reduce the sound with something solid. A closed door will effectively shut some noise out of a room.

The more layers you can put between you and the sound, the less sound will reach you.

Vibrations travel better through hard solids materials than they do through air so pockets of air in a material will help to reduce the sound travelling through that material. Every time the sound
goes from solid to air pocket,
the sound is reduced.

Sponges and foams are soft in structure and have many air pockets so they can be good at absorbing the energy of the sound, thereby muffling it.

What do the children need to know?

You can make a sound quieter by:

- blocking the sound by enclosing the source of the sound, e.g. shutting it in a box or closing the door to reduce the sound coming out of a room;

- moving away from it.

Some materials are good at muffling the sound.

INVESTIGATION: Materials that reduce the sound

You will need:

- a room with thick walls and a sturdy door that can be closed
- pillows or cushions
- a variety of materials including some soft foams/sponges, bubble wrap, and fabric and other materials such as foil and paper and net (make sure you include some holey ones)
- cardboard boxes
- cake tins and plastic boxes with lids (may have to be large – see below)
- a sound maker such as an egg timer that beeps or another device that makes a constant noise – if you have iPads or tablets then you can find a tick tock sound effect on YouTube. These are ideal as they relate beautifully to the story but you'll need big enough boxes to fit them inside.

 # Storify the science

Read the story up to the part where Daddy Bear ends up in the living room and is sitting with his head under a pillow.

Ask the children why he's got a pillow on his head. Elicit that this is because he's trying to block out the sound.

Ask them what they might do in Mr Bear's situation. Give them time to talk to a partner about it. Try their ideas.

If they suggest putting the clock (sound maker) further away or out of the room then get a child to take it outside of the room to see whether you can still hear it. Try with the door open and closed. Try putting a cushion over it. If you let the child who made the suggestion test it out then you'll soon have plenty of suggestions!

 # Set the challenge

You are going to find a way to reduce the sound of that ticking clock (or sound maker) so that Mr Bear can sleep.

You can use any of the items we have provided. You can wrap it, or box it up, or both.

Think about what might work best before you start.

Keep testing until you find a way to make the noise as quiet as possible, without putting it outside the room.

What did you choose? Why?

 # Teacher's top tips

The important skills here are choosing and testing and then improving upon an idea so give them plenty of time to try different materials.

Talk all the time about the materials and why they have selected a particular one. Encourage the children to feel the materials and observe them closely, and to describe what they observe.

The children will find that they need to wrap up the sound maker with lots of layers and put it in the box. If the sound is quite loud then they may not be able to block it altogether and may only be able to make it quieter. Ideally, you want the sound maker to be quiet enough to block the sound out altogether, which will be a clearer result for the children.

If you have younger children and want to run this activity in a more free-flow way, read the story using a clock, blankets and cushions to tell the story and then make those items available for play afterwards. Observe the children playing with the objects as they try to muffle the sound of the clock.

KEY QUESTIONS to help children to move towards an understanding:

- What do you want to try?
- Can you describe this one?
- Which one is better?
- How do you know?
- Is there anything else like that?
- What else would you like to try?
- How will you do it?
- Do you think it will work?

Little extras

If you have a data logger with a sound meter and a big screen in your room, hook up the data logger to detect sound and leave the graph showing the sound levels on the big screen. Don't say anything about it. Just leave it running as the children come in to sit down. The sound levels will go up and down as they make noise.

One or two of the children will notice that their actions make the levels go up and down and start making noises to test this out. Harness this curiosity and ask them why they are making noises. Discuss ideas and try them as a class (you may want to turn it off while you discuss to stop them trying out their own noises while you are have the discussion).

Try being quiet. Try being loud. How high can you make it go? How low? Can you get it to go down to zero? Talk about how loud sounds are bad for our ears. Try testing their ideas from the previous activity, using the data logger's sound meter, and see who managed to reduce the sound most effectively.

What next?

If you want to record your findings in a creative way then you could:

* Ages 4–5: learn a poem or song to share what you did, e.g.:

    > Mr Bear had a noisy clock.
    > Every night it went TICK TOCK
    > It ticked and tocked and wouldn't stop
    > Mr Bear put pillows on top
    > 1 pillow, 2 pillows, 3 then four
    > Now he can't hear it anymore!

* Record a video of each child/group placing the sound maker into the wrapping/box so that the viewer can hear the sound level go down. Encourage the child to say that their idea has made the sound quieter and explain how they think it happened in their own words.

* Write an extra page of the book, storytelling how Mr Bear tried to reduce the sound of the clock. He could try two unsuccessful methods and then find one that works, following the traditional rule of three. It might sound something like this:

    > Page 1 – Mr Bear wrapped it in foil. Tick Tock went the clock.
    >
    > Page 2 – Mr Bear wrapped it in a big box. Tick Tock went the clock.
    >
    > Page 3 – Mr Bear put two cushions in the box and sealed it up tight.
    >
    > Page 4 – Peace at last!

    You could provide a writing frame for those who are not ready to write as much as this. Or, for early writers, write the story together as a class and pin it up in the classroom.

* Role-play being Baby Bear telling Mr Bear how to stop the ticking. Write instructions for Mr Bear so he can remember what to do next time?

Look out for evidence of scientific thinking and learning

* The children carefully listen to the sounds.
* The children think of their own ideas of what to try.
* The children find ways to muffle the sounds.
* The children make observations, e.g. the cake tin made the sound buzzy not quiet.
* The children make links, e.g. when I put the hood up on my coat, I can't hear much so can I try using that?
* The children ask questions, e.g. is it louder with the box open?
* The children test ideas to find answers, e.g. I tried listening to the sound maker in an open box and a closed box and the closed one was quieter.
* The children can sort the materials into materials that are good for muffling the sound and those that are not.

WATERY NOISES

Story link

The dripping tap is noisy.

THE SCIENCE: Some materials make a loud noise when tapped

When you strike an object, such as a drumskin, you cause it to vibrate which in turn vibrates the air around it. The harder you strike the object, the more energy you give the object and the bigger the vibrations you cause and the louder the sound you will hear.

If you strike a soft object, such as a sponge or pillow, the object deforms. Most of the energy you provide goes into deforming the pillow rather than causing it to vibrate and thereby making sound. If you hit it harder, it deforms more, so the most sound you can get out of it is a dull thud.

What do the children need to know?

*   Some materials will make a loud sound when they are struck while others will make a quieter sound.

INVESTIGATION: Investigating dripping noises

You will need:

*   plastic pipettes – 1 per child (cheap to buy through educational suppliers)
*   pots of water
*   plenty of objects to test that could be found in a kitchen sink, e.g. wooden spoons, metal spoons, brillo pads, cloths, sieves, pots and pans, foil trays, china cups and plastic cups, washing up bowls, cooking utensils, metal baking sheets
*   plastic trays to catch the drips.

Storify the science

Look carefully at the kitchen page in the book. Talk about all the objects around the sink and practise the names of the ones that are less familiar to the children, e.g. fish slice or spatula.

Show the children the pipettes and how to use them by squeezing out the air and submerging the tip under water to refill it. Then show them how to make the pipettes drip one drop at a time.

Ask if any children have ever noticed the noise rain makes on a roof. Is it noisier in some rooms? They may be aware that rain is very noticeable on caravan roofs or in portacabin classrooms.

Drip water into a washing-up bowl of water and see if you can hear the sound. If you have a metal sink in your classroom, drip the water directly onto the metal to see what volume of sound can be produced.

Ask the children which one would be loud enough to keep Mr Bear awake.

 # Set the challenge

You are going to pretend to be the leaky kitchen tap so that you can find out which objects would make the most noise in the sink.

First, you need to practise making the pipette drip one drip at a time.

Now try dripping the water onto each object. Listen for the sound it makes.

Can you sort them into objects that make loud sounds that would keep Mr Bear awake and quiet sounds that Mr Bear might not hear?

 # Teacher's top tips

The important skills here are learning to use scientific equipment accurately, making careful observations with our ears and grouping the objects.

Using a pipette is great for fine motor skill control so encourage really accurate dripping to get the most out of this investigation.

There is always the risk that pipettes can be used as water guns so set clear ground rules and tolerate no nonsense!

The results will depend on the items you provide. Metal trays tend to give nice big sounds. Sponges are almost silent. Allow the children to group the objects in the way they see fit as long as they can justify their ideas.

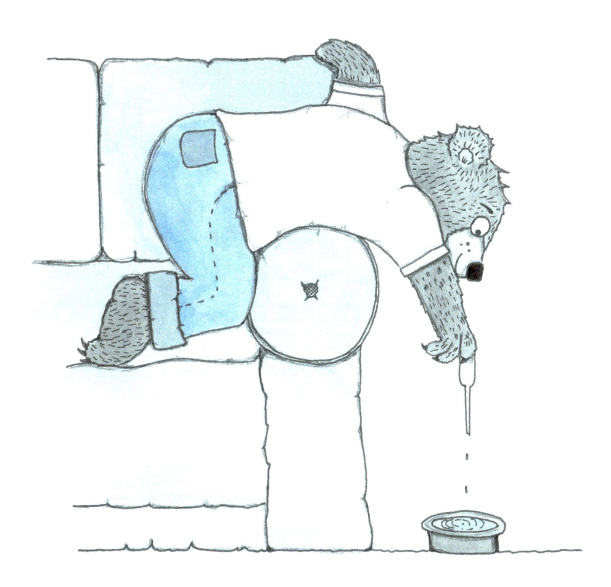

KEY QUESTIONS to help children to move towards an understanding:

- What do you want to try?
- Can you describe this one?
- Which one is louder?
- What else would you like to try?
- What do you think it will sound like?
- Why do you think it will sound like that?

 # What next?

If you want to record your findings in a creative way then you could:

- Ages 4–5: use two washing up bowls to sort the items. You could put all the objects that make a loud sound into one bowl and the ones that make a very quiet sound into another. Take a photo of your sorting and annotate it with an appropriate label for each group.
- Use what you have found out to choose the noisiest items to make a 'kitchen drum kit' (with lolly sticks for sticks) and play it to show what loud noises you can make. You could even play along to 'I am a music man' as you sing as a class.
- Draw a picture of Mr Bear unable to sleep in the kitchen and include a large washing-up bowl containing the objects that made the loudest noises. Label them all. Make poor old Mr Bear look really fed up and tired.
- Role-play being Mr Bear. Tell Mrs Bear about the leaky kitchen tap and how it dripped on all the objects. Show her all the things you found that made a loud noise when they are dripped upon.

 # Look out for evidence of scientific thinking and learning

- The children make observations, e.g. the sponge didn't make any sound!
- The children make links, e.g. all the metal things were really noisy.
- The children ask questions, e.g. if I drip from higher up will it be louder?
- The children make predictions, e.g. I think this one will be quiet like that one.
- The children test ideas to find answers, e.g. the cloth made a quiet sound but it was wet. I'm going to try a dry cloth.
- The children can sort the materials into those that make a loud sound when dripped upon and those that don't.

SOUNDS IN THE GARDEN AT NIGHT

Story link

The garden is noisy.

 THE SCIENCE: Using our ears to identify sounds

Humans use all their senses to perceive the world around them. Using only one sense at a time can make it much harder to accurately work out what is going on.

Little extras for teachers!

Amazingly, if we lose the use of one sense, our brains can learn to compensate. People who have lost their sight can learn to use sound to help them find their way around. Check out the story of Daniel Kish on the internet. He has learned to find his way around by listening to the echoes of click sounds that he makes. Much like a bat, he can echolocate. Astonishingly, the part of his brain that would normally process the sense of sight (the visual cortex) has been shown to be involved when he uses echolocation. Fascinating!

What do the children need to know?

- We hear with our ears but it is hard to identify everything with just one sense. Blind people rely more heavily on the senses of sound and touch.

 ACTIVITY: Identifying sounds in the garden

You will need:

- sound recorders – this could be an App on an iPad or tablet. If you use the video setting, you can listen first to the sounds and then watch the video to see whether you were right
- outside area to visit, if possible.

 Storify the science

Re-read the page about all the noises in the garden. Linger over each sound and make the noises with the children.

Now encourage them to look outside the classroom doors and suggest what they might hear in the school garden today. Open the door/windows. Sit really quietly and see how many sounds you can hear.

Ask the children whether they think that everyone can hear the same things. Discuss that some sounds are so quiet that only people who are very near them might hear them.

Ask the children whether they think they could identify animals by the sound they make. Discuss the fact that we know what noises many familiar farm animals make but we are unlikely to get a pig in the school garden. Do we know how to tell the difference between a robin and a sparrow? Do snails make a sound?

Ask the children whether they could tell who was coming by the footsteps they make. Discuss being blind and how else you might know who was present, e.g. by their voice or their perfume.

Ask the children how good they think they would be at identifying things (in the garden) by their sounds alone.

 # Set the challenge

You are going to collect five sounds from the school garden (or from the school building if you prefer). You are going to record them and then we will listen to them and see if we can identify them.

You might need to do something to make the sound. Try to choose things to do that happen in everyday life. People may not be able to identify a sound they haven't heard before, e.g. banging a welly with a spoon!

You could try footsteps on different surfaces, bells or whistles, bouncing balls, rustling leaves, toy cars trundling, or gates and doors squeaking as they open! I'm sure you'll have some great ideas of your own to surprise us with.

Try not to record people talking, so remember to be quiet once you have pressed record.

Now play your sounds to someone. Can they guess what made the sound?

Were they all easy to recognise? Why?

 # Teacher's top tips

The important skills here are choosing the best sounds to record and making careful observations with our ears. Encourage the children to think about the sounds they want to record.

It is quite hard to tell some sounds apart such as footsteps on gravel and scrunching up paper. Spend time discussing which other senses would help you in these situations.

There are lots of sound identifying games on the internet. So if your school is in a built-up area and you'd like to listen to sounds from the countryside, you can find them already recorded and use those.

Children think it is hilarious to record bathroom noises so set the ground rules about where they are allowed to record before you start, to avoid inappropriate behaviour!

KEY QUESTIONS to help children to move towards an understanding:

- What do you want to try?
- How shall we do it?
- Can you describe this one?
- Which one is easier to recognise?
- What might be really tricky to recognise?
- Does that sound the same?
- What did that sound like?

What next?

If you want to record your findings in a creative way then you could:

- Ages 4–5: play a game with your collected sounds. Make up an action for each sound. Listen for the sounds and the last person to do the action is out!
- Draw yourself in the garden surrounded by the sounds you heard.
- Make a little book about the sounds you heard. Draw an object or animal you heard on each page. You could have the words 'I can hear____'. pre-written on each page, if needed. You could even make a tally chart to show how many times you heard each sound in 5 minutes of sitting quietly in the garden.
- Write a new page for the story book about the sounds you found in the school garden today. You could even begin with the phrase 'You wouldn't believe what noises there are in our school garden today'. Choose some interesting words to describe the noises you heard, e.g. scrunch went the gravel!
- Draw a picture of the school garden. On small pieces of paper, draw the things you recorded and stick them as lift-up-flaps on to your picture of the school garden, in the right places. Under the flaps, write the sounds they made.

Look out for evidence of scientific thinking and learning

- The children have their own ideas about what sounds to collect.
- The children make observations, e.g. it was hard to guess the gravel sound.
- The children ask questions, e.g. how does a deaf person know when someone is at the door?
- The children test ideas to find answers, e.g. wiping my feet on the doormat sounds like walking on the path. Let's record both and see whether people can hear the difference.

_____

SHH . . . LET'S HELP MR BEAR SLEEP

Story link

Mrs Bear is concerned about Mr Bear.

THE SCIENCE: Making noises quieter

You'll find everything you need to know about making sounds quieter earlier in this chapter on p. 34.

INVESTIGATION: Making ear defenders

You will need:

- normal sized paper cups for coffee (two per child)
- soft materials that will muffle sounds, e.g. foam, fleece, furry fabrics, sponge, bubblewrap, cotton wool, cornstarch packaging
- materials that won't muffle sounds, e.g. wooden beads, plastic bricks, foil, netting, card (nothing small enough to fit into ear canals)
- other materials that can be squashed to form a thick barrier, e.g. paper, paper towels
- thin cloth circles for lids
- elastic bands
- bigger cups and smaller cups.

Storify the science

Read the last part of the book where Mr Bear goes back to bed and falls asleep because Mrs Bear isn't snoring anymore and continue to the end. Poor Mr Bear looks tired. Imagine if that happened night after night.

Ask what advice the children might give Mr Bear. They might suggest sleeping in the spare room – relate this to the lesson where you moved the clock further away so the sound was quieter.

They might suggest ear plugs or ear defenders. If not, show the children some ear defenders and ask how they might help Mr Bear.

Ask the children what they think might be inside the ear defenders. Give them time to talk about this with a partner. Encourage all ideas, even the ones you know are unlikely and let them know that they can test out their ideas in the next activity.

Set the challenge

You are going to make some ear defenders. You'll need a paper cup for each ear.

- Try putting the cup over your ear with nothing in it. Does it make the sound of the classroom quieter?

- Remember what we learned about materials that made the clock sound quieter. Can you think of some materials that might muffle the sounds in the classroom?

- Try putting some materials into the cups. Does it make the sound quieter?

- Keep testing until you find the best material for the job.

- Which material was the best at muffling? Is that what you expected?

Teacher's top tips

The important skills here are predicting based on what we learned before, testing and choosing the best material for the job.

Allow plenty of time for testing and encourage testing things to check they don't work.

When children rush the task, ask them to make their design even better (by squishing more material into the cup or choosing a better material).

You want to avoid small bits and pieces falling into ears so you may want to avoid using scissors so that the children have to use the larger pieces that you provide. Alternatively, put a cloth top on the cup, secured with an elastic band before putting the cup to their ears, so that nothing can fall out of the cup into their ears.

The children may need to test their design with a louder sound than classroom noise so you may want to stop the class and test designs every so often by playing music for 30 seconds in the classroom.

You might like to use these cups to make your own ear defenders on a headband so that they stay on.

KEY QUESTIONS to help children to move towards an understanding:

- What do you want to try?
- Why do you think that one will muffle sound?
- Can you describe this one?
- Which one is better?
- How do you know?
- Is there anything else like that?
- What else would you like to try?
- How will you do it?
- Do you think it will work?

What next?

If you want to record your findings in a creative way then you could:

- Ages 4–5: fill a cup with materials that made the noise sound quieter. Fill another cup with materials that didn't. Show your sorting to an adult.
- Make a little book to show what you tried. This could be pre-prepared with pages that read 'I tested _____ . Did it work? ____' Save the one that works for the last page!
- Write an advert for your ear defenders. Draw the design and describe the materials inside the cup. Explain how to use the ear defenders and how they work.
- Role-play a conversation where Baby Bear gives the ear defenders to Mr Bear as a present. Pretend to be Baby Bear and explain how you made them and how they work to Mr Bear.

Look out for evidence of scientific thinking and learning

- The children make their own decisions about what to put in their ear defenders.
- The children make observations, e.g. the soft materials worked really well.
- The children make links, e.g. my ear muffs are soft and squidgy and they make the sound quieter too.
- The children ask questions, e.g. if I used a bigger cup I could get more material in it – would that make it work better?
- The children test ideas to find answers, e.g. can I try a bigger cup?
- The children can sort the materials into those that successfully reduce the sound and those that don't.

---

4   *Traction Man Is Here*

Mini Grey (2006)

TOPIC PLANNER

Story link	Science: Properties of materials	Activity	Page
Accessories for diving (in the sink)	Floating materials Testing and sorting	Making floats for Traction Man Sorting objects and materials to make the best floats for Traction Man (investigation)	51–2
Clothes for jungles	Tough materials Testing and choosing the best for the job	Testing jungle fabrics Testing materials to see which will last longest (investigation)	56–7
Boots for deep sea diving (at the bottom of the bath)	Sinking materials Predicting and testing.	Making diving boots Testing objects and materials to find ones which sink (investigation)	60
Protective suits (in case of falling off the kitchen cliff)	Soft and squashy materials Testing and sorting	Making a protective suit for Scrubbing Brush Testing materials to see which would protect Scrubbing Brush (investigation)	63–4
Ways to help the world with a knitted suit	The many uses of wool	Finding out about wool (activity)	67
Clothes for new places (the fridge)	Materials to stop us losing heat Testing a prediction to find the best material for the job	Making a cold weather suit for Traction Man Testing materials to see which can keep a baked potato warm (investigation)	70

ACCESSORIES FOR DIVING IN THE SINK

Story link

Traction man dives in the sink

THE SCIENCE: Floating materials

To understand why some things float you need to understand density.

Some materials are heavy for their size. A cube of one material can be much heavier than a cube of the exact same size of a different material. The heavier one is more dense.

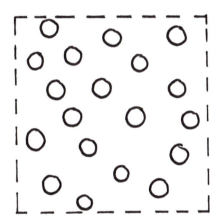 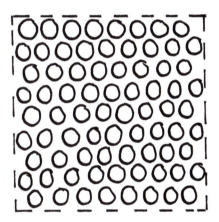

All materials are made from tiny molecules packed together. If they are packed together very tightly, they will be more dense than a material that is less tightly packed. To find the exact density of a material you need to know how heavy each molecule is, how large each molecule is and how closely packed they are. In a very dense material, the molecules would be small and heavy and tightly packed together so there is a lot of stuff in a small space.

Materials float on a liquid if they are less dense than that liquid. Air is much less dense than water so any material that contains pockets of air will be less dense than water and the air pockets will give that material some buoyancy in the water.

Air is a mixture of gases. Molecules of gases are very spread out so they are not very dense at all.

What do the children need to know?

- Some materials float and some sink!

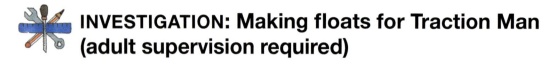

INVESTIGATION: Making floats for Traction Man (adult supervision required)

You will need:

- plastic dolls that sink in the water (or metal spoons with faces drawn on them)
- large tanks of water
- objects and materials that float, e.g. apples, wooden bricks, bubble wrap, ping pong balls, rubber ducks, inflated mini balloons, polystyrene balls, wooden spoons, empty oral syringes (used in pneumatics)
- objects and materials that sink, e.g. modelling clay, leather, solid plastic bricks, stones, potatoes
- tape, string, elastic bands and other joining materials that will stick in wet conditions
- an inflatable arm band (for swimming).

Storify the science

Look carefully at the pages where Traction Man dives in the sink and find all the interesting objects in the pictures. Ask whether the objects in the picture would float or sink – try some in a tank of water that the children can all see, e.g. a metal sieve and a wooden spoon. Discuss the wooden spoon at the bottom of the sink. Is it in the right place in the picture? Put a doll/metal spoon that sinks into the water (solid plastic dolls often sink). Oh no! Our Traction Man is sinking. How could we help him to stay up in the water while he searches for wrecks? Look in the picture for clues about how Traction man is staying up. Show some armbands. Ask the children for ideas about how they work. But the armbands are too big for Traction Man . . .

Set the challenge

You are going to find out which materials could be used to make Traction Man a Floatation Device for Searching for Wrecks.

Have a look at all the equipment. How will you know what is good for making floats?

Test everything to find out which are useful for making a floatation device and then think about how you could make something for Traction Man.

Teacher's top tips

The important skills here are observation and testing out ideas. Don't worry about the product looking realistic. Tying an apple to a doll may make it float in the water so that is a successful float. It doesn't need to look like a floatation device.

Let the children play with the items for a while. Recruit as many dolls that sink as you can to play at being Traction Man so that the children can try getting the dolls to float while tied to an

apple etc. But metal spoons with a permanent marker face could also stand in for Traction Man and are easy to source. And importantly, they sink without a floatation device.

Having time to explore will give the children a chance to see whether all floats work for all dolls and observe whether they all float at the same height in the water. You may want to make this activity available for children to revisit over the course of a few days.

Give the children a chance to tell you what they discovered. Once they have shared their ideas, other children may go away and build upon that idea. So, lots of mini discussions along the way can really help children to progress their learning.

Children often have misconceptions about this topic such as the idea that all heavy things will sink or that small objects will float, or more unusual ones, e.g. toy ducks, will float whatever they are made from. Allowing them to test freely will give them a wider experience to draw upon when spotting the patterns for themselves.

KEY QUESTIONS to help children to move towards an understanding:

- What do you want to try?
- Why did you choose that?
- Can you find some things that float?
- Do they always float? Can you make them sink?
- Do they all float right at the top?
- Are the floating things all the same in some way?
- Are they all big?
- Are they all heavy?

Little extras

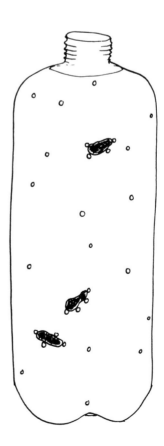

You could have a large bottle of fizzy water in the classroom. It must be open at the top so make sure it won't tip over, and add a few raisins. Let the children discover it. Give them the opportunity to add raisins and observe. Bubbles of carbon dioxide (which has been dissolved in the fizzy water) will form on the raisins and cause them to float to the surface. When the bubbles pop, the raisins sink back to the bottom. Experiencing this sort of thing will give them a chance to make links between the air in an arm-band and the air in the bubble. Allowing them to notice this for themselves, without prompting, can really engage their interest in observing the world around them.

What next?

If you want to record your findings in a creative way then you could:

- Ages 4–5: put all the items that would make a good floatation device into a tray. Stick the one you think is best on to Traction Man with tape.
- Write mini floating facts books. Include some short sentences about the investigation, e.g. metal spoons sink, wooden spoons float.
- Role-play being a floatation device inventor. Advertise your device – you could draw a picture or take a photo of your flotation device and annotate it explaining why the objects/materials you used are perfect for the job.
- Make a TV advert for your floatation device using a digital storytelling app where photographs of models or drawings can be combined with oral explanations and captured in a short film.
- Write an instruction booklet for Traction Man so he can make his own flotation device.

Look out for evidence of scientific thinking and learning

- The children choose their own objects to test.
- The children make observations, e.g. The bubble wrap floats!
- The children make links, e.g. The bubblewrap has air in it and so does the rubber duck.
- The children ask questions, e.g. Does bubblewrap float if you pop it?
- The children come up with their own ideas to try out, e.g. Crayons are the right shape. Can I try a crayon?
- The children test ideas to find answers, e.g. The crayon sank – it won't make a good float.
- The children can sort the materials with reference to floating and sinking.

———————————————

CLOTHES FOR JUNGLES

Story link
Traction Man is in the garden.

THE SCIENCE: Tough materials

When clothes are manufactured there are many considerations. Clothing needs to drape well over the body, it needs to resist stains, insulate the body, stand up to wear and tear and of course it must look good: especially for Traction Man.

In these experiments, we will consider the how easily a fabric can be abraded or even torn by a rough surface. The type of thread and the way it is woven will affect how well it resists fraying or tearing. The threads may be thick or made from many thinner threads twisted together to make the thread tougher. There are many types of fabric used to make clothes. The clothing manufacturers select the best kind of fabric for the job. Denim, made from cotton, was developed for farm workers to be tough and hard wearing. Nowadays, water resistant, lightweight fabrics can also be made from tough synthetic fibres so that outdoor clothes are lighter and better in the rain. You can test any fabrics you can gather. The important thing is to link the material to its suitability for its purpose.

What do the children need to know?

- Clothes for rough environments need to be made from tough fabric.
- Fabrics are made from different kinds of thread and they all have different properties.

 ## INVESTIGATION: Testing jungle fabrics

- sandpaper
- rocks (smooth and craggy)
- scrubbing brushes
- brillo pads
- hand lenses
- a variety of pieces of material for testing, e.g. denim, satin, cotton, canvas, kitchen towel, washing up cloths, leather, silk.

 ## Storify the science

Set up a miniature assault course in a tray for a washable plastic doll. Include a cheese grater and some rocks and a sieve to climb. Read the page where Traction Man rescues the dolls from the flower bed. Take the doll (Traction Girl/Boy) through the assault course and get it all muddy and (if you don't mind the sacrifice) rip some of the clothing. Be dismayed! Ask the children to explain to the doll why the clothes are ripped. Discuss what our parents say when we are going out to play outside in our best clothes. Which clothes are best for outside?

 ## Set the challenge

You are going to find out which material would be best to make a Tough Outdoor Top for Traction Man.

You'll need to look closely at the fabrics. Use your eyes and your fingers.

Try using some of the equipment to wear a hole in the fabric.

Think which fabric Traction Man should choose for his Tough Outdoor Top. Remember he needs to be comfy too.

Think about:

*   which fabrics wear out quickly;
*   which fabrics are hard to tear;
*   how to test each fabric.

Make a Tough Outdoor Top for Traction Man! (This could be a gillet made from a rectangle with two holes cut for the arms or a rectangle with a central hole for the head which can be worn as a tabard with a string belt.)

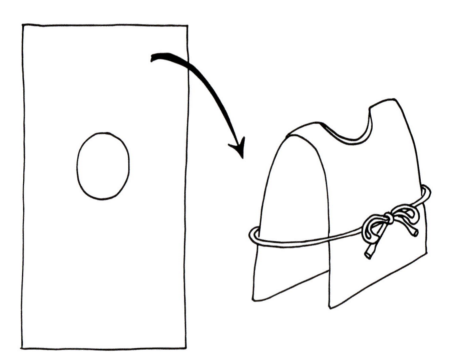

 # Teacher's top tips

The important skills here are observing the fabrics before and after trying to wear holes in them.

Make sure you include pieces of fabric for testing that will be easily abraded by the sandpaper and rocks etc. as little hands aren't always strong enough to damage cottons. Fabrics such as satin, lining fabric or silks are very thin. The fibres are delicate and will catch and pucker and rip.

Once the children have found a tough fabric, encourage the children to make their own garments for Traction Man. It doesn't matter what they look like. Only get involved when materials are hard to cut or when fingers might get hurt. A length of fabric wrapped and tied around a doll will still show a child's choice of fabric.

If you have a hand held digital microscope you can look at the fabrics really closely, before and after the children abrade them with the sandpaper and rocks. You should see a real difference in the amount of fibres that are fluffy and frayed.

KEY QUESTIONS to help children to move towards an understanding:

- What do you want to try?
- What can you see with the magnifier?
- What can you feel?
- What is the same about the fabrics? What is different?
- How shall we find out if it is tough?
- Do all the fabrics do that?
- Can you find a tougher one?
- Are there any fabrics you think won't be tough? How do you know?

The children may come up with a question, e.g. Does it break when it is wet? Does the mud protect it? If you can see a way to try to find an answer to the question in the classroom then encourage them to find their own answer, fetching them the equipment they will need. This is the purpose of scientific enquiry: to help children to notice something about the world around them and to ask their own questions and find their own answers through testing.

What next?

If you want to record your findings in a creative way then you could:

- Ages 4–5: provide a drawing of Traction Man in a white generic outfit so that the children can stick on a piece of the fabric they would choose and label the fabric with descriptive phrases such as 'thick cotton' or 'it didn't wear out'.
- Draw a design for a Tough Outfit for Jungles, giving each garment a good name and sticking on swatches of the fabrics you would use for each part.
- Choose clothes to make a Tough Outfit for Jungles and dress up as Traction Man. Tell someone why you chose the clothes you are wearing or take a photograph and write about your outfit.
- Role-play being Traction Man talking to Scrubbing Brush or another toy. There are dolls in the garden to rescue but Traction Man isn't dressed yet. Talk about which clothes he should put on.

Look out for evidence of scientific thinking and learning

- The children use their senses to explore the fabrics.
- The children make observations, e.g. this material has tiny threads.
- The children make links, e.g. the thick fabrics are hard to damage.
- The children ask questions, e.g. why doesn't this material have lines?
- The children can sort the materials into those that are easily abraded and those that can withstand it.

_____

BOOTS FOR DEEP SEA DIVING

Story link

Traction Man is in the bath.

THE SCIENCE: Sinking materials

If a material is more dense than water it will sink when placed in water (see p. 51).

What do the children need to know?

- Some materials sink while others float.

INVESTIGATION: Making diving boots (adult supervision required)

You will need:

- plastic dolls that float in the water (wooden spoons with faces drawn on)
- large tanks of water
- objects and materials that float, e.g. corks, lolly sticks, pumice, empty oral syringes
- objects and materials that sink, e.g. cotton reels, playdough, small metal weights, spoons, marbles, chalk, pebbles
- interesting materials that can float or sink, such as sponge
- tape, string, elastic bands and other joining materials that will stick in wet conditions.

Storify the science

Read the pages about diving to the bottom of the bath. Put a doll/wooden spoon that floats into a tank of water so that all the children can see it. Drop some glass beads or other 'treasure' into the tank. Push the doll down towards the treasure explaining that Traction Man wants to retrieve the treasure from the bottom. Let go and watch the doll bob back up. Discuss ways to help Traction Man get to the bottom. Look back in the book. What does Traction Man wear in the book? What do diving boots do? Would it be better to have a heavy diving hat or heavy diving gloves instead? Could we find something to make diving boots for our doll?

Set the challenge

You are going to test some of these materials and objects. Which material do you think will be best to make Boots for Deep-Sea Diving for our doll?

You'll need to test the objects and find out which will keep a diver at the bottom of the sea. You could even make boots.

Think about:

- how to test each material;
- what to look for;
- which material would make good boots.

Was your first idea correct?

 # Teacher's top tips

The important skills here are observation, predicting and testing. The children will be familiar with the idea of floating and sinking so introduce plenty of new items to test. Make sure some materials are easy to mould or tie onto the doll/wooden spoon so that boots can be made.

Encourage the children to try attaching the weights to different parts of the doll to see what happens. The heaviest part will end up lowest in the water so a heavy diving helmet would hold the doll upside down.

Don't leave deep water tanks unattended. Clear water tanks on a table are best. then no one can fall in.

KEY QUESTIONS to help children to move towards an understanding:

- What do you want to try?
- What might be good for boots? How do you know?
- How shall we fix it to the doll?
- Where shall we fix it on the doll?
- Does it work?
- Could you find something better?

 # What next?

If you want to record your findings in a creative way then you could:

- Ages 4–5: provide pictures of the items available for testing and a large picture of a tank of water. Encourage the children to stick the items that float at the top and the others at the bottom to show what they found out. You could include a drawing of Traction Man so they can stick their chosen item to his feet for his boots.

- Draw a postcard of things Traction Man might find at the bottom of the sea. Only include items that would sink to the bottom.

- Design a pair of diving boots and draw the box to sell them in. Write a description of your boots to go on the box, detailing your design.

Look out for evidence of scientific thinking and learning

- The children make observations, e.g. The metal weights sink right to the bottom.

- The children make predictions, e.g. I think the metal weights will make good diving boots.

- The children make links, e.g. Most of the heavy things sink well.

- The children ask questions, e.g. My flip flop floated away in the sea. Would a wellie float too?

- The children test ideas to find answers, e.g. When my wellie filled with water it sank.

- The children can sort the materials into those that sink and those that don't. They may be able to identify air pockets in some of the materials that float.

PROTECTIVE SUITS

Story link

Traction Man and Scrubbing Brush are very high up.

THE SCIENCE: Soft and squashy materials

If you fall from a high place you would hit the ground hard. When we hit something we apply a force to it.

Forces can make things move, change the speed of something already moving or cause something to change shape.

If you push a toy car you apply a push force to it and it might move forward.

If you put your hand on a moving car you could apply a force to stop it moving.

If you land on a soft material then that material will change shape and slow the landing. Imagine jumping into a huge marshmallow – you would create a big dent in the middle.

The marshmallow absorbs the impact and you wouldn't get hurt. This is because the marshmallow can change shape and slows down how quickly you stop. This means that you do not experience a large force on your body. If that soft material is also springy like foam then it might bounce back into shape again when you get off.

If you land on a hard material that cannot change shape you may cause bones to break and soft tissues to bruise. This is because your body is slowed down very quickly and experiences a very large force. This is why we wear crash helmets, on our bikes, which can absorb the force of impact by changing shape, by being crushed, so that our heads are not hurt.

It is how quickly that you come to stop that determines whether you get hurt or not.

What do the children need to know?

- Soft, spongy or crushable materials can protect us from being hurt when we fall on them.

 ## INVESTIGATION: Making a protective suit for Scrubbing Brush

You will need:

- an old cycle helmet
- trays of modelling bricks
- modelling dough
- soft spongy materials, e.g. thick fleece, bubblewrap, tissue (crumpled), corrugated cardboard boxes, sponge, craft foam sheets
- thin materials, e.g. satin, thin card, tissue, paper.

 ## Storify the science

Read the pages of the story where Traction Man and Scrubbing Brush rescue the spoons from the Broom. Look at the picture of brave little Scrubbing Brush jumping down to save the spoons. Traction Man didn't have time to think about it and Scrubbing Brush was very brave but he might not want to jump like that again. What could have happened to him? Discuss the bumps and bruises that the children have had in their lives. Ask if they would want to jump off the Kitchen Cliff without protection. Look at the cycle helmet – discuss the design and the materials used to help prevent injury.

Show the children a modelling dough model of Scrubbing Brush. Hold it at a height above a tray full of spoons and modelling bricks. What might happen? Drop the dough – observe and discuss what happens, relating it to human bodies being damaged. Roll the model into a smooth ball with no dents. Show the children some of the available materials Traction Man could wrap around Scrubbing Brush. Ask which he should choose.

Set the challenge

You are going to find out which materials would keep Scrubbing Brush safe on his journey over the Kitchen Cliff. Roll up a ball of modelling dough into a nice round ball. Place the material over a tray of bricks. Try dropping it onto the different materials. See if your dough gets dented or not to see which material would stop Scrubbing Brush getting any bruises.

Think about:

- how to make sure you drop it from the same height every time;
- how you arrange the material to make it as soft a landing as possible.

Remember to smooth out any dents in the dough before each test.

Which material would be safest for Scrubbing Brush to land on?

Teacher's top tips

The important skills here are observation and testing. Allow the children to try out their ideas. You may also want to focus on the skill of planning the test and allow them to work out their own method of making it as fair as possible rather than providing specific instructions. N.B. small children understand the concept of cheating even if they don't understand the idea of making a test fair so you might use the term 'testing without cheating'.

There is no need for measuring. The children can observe the dents in the dough then retest a material in thicker layers, folded or scrunched. It is easy to set up and can be left out, to be revisited later.

Some materials will absorb lots of the force if it is thickly layered whereas thick card will tend to dent the dough as the card is hard and won't change shape to absorb the force.

You may want to place some kind of marker on the wall near the tray to encourage the children to drop the ball from the same height.

Once the children have decided which material is best, you could have a class testing session where you remake the modelling dough model of Scrubbing Brush and wrap him in different materials and see which material protects him most effectively from a fall.

KEY QUESTIONS to help children to move towards an understanding:

- What are you going to do?
- How will you make it the same each time (i.e. no cheating)?
- What are you going to look for?
- What would you want to fall onto if it was you? Why?
- What does it feel like?
- Do all the soft things work well?

Afterwards, revisit the cycling helmet and reinforce the importance of safety clothing for humans too.

What next?

If you want to record your findings in a creative way then you could:

*   Ages 4–5: stick your chosen material over a picture of Scrubbing Brush to show it would protect him well.
*   Create a catalogue of *Protective Coats for Brave Pets*. Draw and label coats of the different materials that would provide protection from injury. Or you could provide pictures of the different materials or even glue in pieces of the materials.
*   Make a leaflet for Traction Man advertising the protective coat you would make for Scrubbing Brush.
*   Take a photo of the dough when dented by the bricks with no protective coat and one when the dough had been protected by the material. Write a letter to Traction Man telling him he must take care of his pet and suggest ways he could do this based on your research.
*   Role-play being Traction Man explaining to Scrubbing Brush why he should wear his protective suit.

Look out for evidence of scientific thinking and learning

*   The children find their own way to solve the problem.
*   The children make observations, e.g. the corners of the bricks go into the dough.
*   The children plan their own test, e.g. I'm going to push the dough off the edge of the same table each time.
*   The children make links, e.g. the soft, fluffy materials stop the dough getting dented.
*   The children ask questions, e.g. what are my football pads made from? How do they protect me? Would they protect the dough?
*   The children test ideas to find answers, e.g. the cushions are soft to sit on and they stopped the dough from getting dented when I tested it.
*   The children can sort the materials into those that will protect the Scrubbing Brush and those that won't. They may be able to generalise about the materials that work well, e.g. the soft squishy materials that bounce back when you press them make good protective coats.
*   The children can review their protective coat and say whether it worked well or not.

———————————

WAYS TO HELP THE WORLD WITH A KNITTED SUIT

Story link
Traction man's suit unravels.

THE SCIENCE: The many uses of wool

Wool is made from tiny fibres twisted together. Each fibre itself is not very strong but because the strand of wool is made from many fibres, their combined strength is considerable. Combining more strands will make the wool stronger still.

What do the children need to know?

- Wool is made from fibres twisted together to make them stronger.

ACTIVITY: Finding out about wool

You will need:

- wool of different thicknesses
- short lengths of wool (1 each)
- string
- rope
- magnifying glasses

- things to thread, e.g. beads, straws, binca with large holes, cotton reels
- instructions for tying knots
- squares of knitting that can be unravelled
- simple cardboard box looms for weaving.

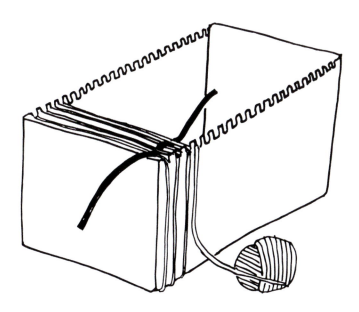

Storify the science

Return to the page where Traction Man's green romper suit is beginning to unravel and Scrubbing Brush gets the idea to use the wool to rescue the spoons. Look closely at the drawings. Can you see the detail on the wool? Look at wool, string and rope with magnifying glasses or better still a hand held magnifier connected to a smart board. Ask them if they can see what the strand of wool is made from. Discuss how the wool is twisted. Ask the children to think about why it is twisted. Give out short lengths for the children to look at. Give them time to talk to a partner about what they see. Untwist some wool and find the strands. Demonstrate breaking individual strands and then try the same with thick twists of wool. Ask the children what they notice. Discuss the thickness of the strand and how that relates to the strength of the strand. Ask the children to come up with other useful things Traction Man could do with the wool from his romper suit.

 # Set the challenge

You are going to find as many ways as you can to use wool to do something useful. You can knot it, knit it, weave it, plait it, combine it with other items and add the useful things to our display with a label explaining your useful item for Traction Man. You could make a bag with a strong handle. You might want to try making a strong belt or a lead for scrubbing brush.

Think about:

- the ways to make the wool stronger;
- the equipment Traction Man might need to rescue other toys.

 # Teacher's top tips

The important skills here are exploring the materials and being creative. There is no right or wrong answer. Give the children time to play and come up with things they could make for Traction Man.

Provide plenty of interesting materials and objects to help them come up with ideas.

They might suggest Traction Man could make a lead for the Scrubbing Brush. They might make a belt or a bag from the binca with a woollen handle. Celebrate all their ideas. The ideas don't have to be perfect, beautiful or even practical as long as they are using the wool and finding ways to twist or plait the wool to make it into thicker threads.

If you can persuade a parent to knit you a romper suit for your classroom Traction Man in green then put him on display with slightly trailing toes. Also provide little patches of knitting that can be unravelled to explore knitting. You may find a patient parent who will come into school and demonstrate or even teach interested children to knit to make wool into fabric that could be made into useful items for Traction Man.

Some of your children may find this task so wide open that they don't know where to start. You may want to make a few items yourself so that they can be copied or adapted by these children, e.g. a bag, a lead, a belt, a lasso, a climbing rope, a hammock, a rope ladder, etc.

What next?

If you want to record your findings in a creative way then you could:

- Ages 4–5: set up a shop of the things you have made for Traction Man to visit. Write labels for the items in the shop.
- Role-play Traction Man going shopping at your 'Useful Items Made from Wool' shop. Maybe Granny is the shopkeeper. Talk about the items in the shop and why they might be useful.
- Write instruction booklets on how to make the items you made so that others can make them too.
- Explain your item on a short film to send to Traction Man. You could show him how to make it and how it should be used or worn.

Look out for evidence of scientific thinking and learning

- The children engage with this open-ended activity.
- The children think of their own ideas.
- The children make observations, e.g. you can unwind the wool!
- The children make links, e.g. the string and the rope unwind too.
- The children ask questions, e.g. is the thread stronger than the wool?
- The children test ideas to find answers e.g. will the thickest wool be hardest to break? I couldn't break the blue wool so I'll use that to make a lead for his pet.
- The children manage to twist or plait the wool to make stronger strands.
- The children make a functional item for Traction Man.

———————————

CLOTHES FOR NEW PLACES

Story link

Where might Traction Man go next?

 THE SCIENCE: Materials to stop us losing heat

Just like all warm-blooded animals, our bodies produce heat. We use the energy from our food to create this heat. Our hair and our clothes trap a layer of warm air around our bodies to stop our bodies losing heat.

Certain materials are good at trapping layers of warm air. They slow down how fast heat is lost from the body. We call them good thermal insulators.

This process can happen in reverse. When we use a cool bag to keep our food cool we trap layers of cool air around the food using thermal insulators which slows down how fast heat from the outside can reach the cold food.

Fluffy fibres such as wool and fleece make great thermal insulators. They will slow down heat loss from our bodies and, if wrapped around an ice cream, would prevent the heat from the outside reaching the ice cream and melting it.

What do the children need to know?

- Some materials will keep us warm by trapping the warm air inside.

 INVESTIGATION: Making a cold weather suit for Traction Man

You will need:

- warm (not hot) baked potatoes under adult supervision
- a variety of different fabrics to test, including fleece and netting
- a fridge.

Storify the science

Imagine the kitchen where Traction Man lives. Where else could he visit? Imagine and talk about the possible perils of the oven, the microwave, the cat flap and the fridge. Explain that you are going to make up another adventure for Traction Man. This time someone/something needs rescuing from the fridge. Discuss what could be lost in the fridge and need rescuing by Traction Man. Come up with a simple storyline where Traction Man must go into the fridge to perform a rescue. (If you can build in some of the string inventions from last week, all the better.) But Scrubbing Brush is worried he will get cold and makes him dress up in his Thermal Suit for keeping warm in Arctic Places.

 # Set the challenge

You are going to choose the best material for making a Thermal Suit for Arctic Places. We are going to use a warm potato instead of a person and see if we can keep the potato warm. Look at all the fabrics. Feel them and decide which one will keep the potato warm. Choose something to wrap the warm potato in and then put your wrapped potato into the fridge.

We are going to leave the potato there for 20 minutes.

After 20 minutes, we will open up the potato and see whether the insides are still warm. You could do this by pushing a thermometer into a little hole in the potato skin or your adult helper could feel the inside with their fingers.

Did your choice of material keep the potato warm?

 # Teacher's top tips

The important skill here is prediction. They children only get one chance to test so they need to spend time making sensible predictions beforehand. They will have some idea of what warm clothes feel like so they may well make good choices but provide options that won't keep a potato warm too.

Obviously, you need to be safe so use potatoes that are warm to touch but not hot enough to burn as the potato may be dropped and scatter the contents everywhere.

You can draw faces on the potato so it feels more like a person.

Before the lesson, try putting a warm baked potato in the fridge without any wrapper and keep checking so you can see how long it takes to cool in your particular fridge. You may need to take the potatoes out after less time if your fridge is very efficient.

Children often assume that the clothes themselves somehow give heat to the wearer rather than reducing heat loss from an already warm body. They therefore assume that putting a coat on a snowman would make it melt. In real life, the coat would trap cold air inside, preventing the heat reaching the snow inside the coat and keeping the snow cold and solid. This is a misconception common among older children so don't worry if they don't fully grasp the idea at this first investigation into thermal insulation.

KEY QUESTIONS to help children to move towards an understanding:

- What does it feel like in the fridge?
- Which is warmer – the potato or the fridge?
- What would you want to wear if you had to go to a cold place?
- What do you think will happen?
- What would you like to try?
- What does it feel like?
- Why did you choose it?
- Is there anything that will be better?

 # What next?

If you want to record your findings in a creative way then you could:

- Ages 4–5: dress up in clothes that would keep you warm on an artic adventure. Take a photo.
- Send a postcard from Traction Man in the Arctic Fridge. On the front you could draw him in his Thermal Suit. You could write a message to Scrubbing Brush telling him what his suit is made of and whether it is keeping him warm.
- Role-play a new adventure called Traction Man and the daring rescue from the Artic Fridge. Write your story down and include a sentence about the suit he wears.

 # Look out for evidence of scientific thinking and learning

- The children choose which fabric to test.
- The children make observations, e.g. the potato is cold now!
- The children make simple predictions, e.g. I think the woolly scarf material will keep him warm.
- The children make links, e.g. my coat is really thick and my warm jumper is really thick too.
- The children ask questions, e.g. is your thin fleece warm?
- The children test ideas to find answers, e.g. I think the fleece is warm even though it is thin so I'm going to try that.
- The children can sort the materials into those that will be good for a Thermal Suit for keeping warm in Arctic Places and those that won't.

5 *The Storm Whale in Winter*
(A cold weather topic)
Benji Davies (2016)

TOPIC PLANNER

Story link	Science: Ice – melting and freezing	Activity	Page
Snow	Observing snow Testing Comparing and describing materials	Which is the best sort of snow? Making different kinds of snow – which one feels most like real snow? (activity)	74
Exploring ice	Ice forms on top of the water Testing ideas Reviewing whether the idea worked	Making an ice bridge Tinkering with ice and water to see whether we can make an ice bridge (activity)	79
Does everything freeze?	Freezing other liquids Generating ideas Observing what happens	Solidifying liquids Freezing different liquids (investigation)	85
Rescuing the boat	Investigating melting ice	Ways to melt the ice Melting/breaking lumps of ice in different ways (activity)	88–9

SNOW

Story link

Winter was setting in.

THE SCIENCE: Snow

Snow is formed when the temperature is so low that the water vapour in the air cools, not to liquid droplets in a cloud, but tiny ice crystals. These crystals clump together to form snowflakes when they bump into one another. When the snowflake is sufficiently big and heavy it will fall to the ground: it will snow.

If the temperature of the air remains below 0 °C, the snowflakes fall as 'dry snow' which drifts easily and is good for skiing.

If the temperature of the air is slightly warmer, a little over 0°C, then the snowflakes melt around the edges and stick together to make 'wet snow' that clumps together and is great for building snowmen.

What do the children need to know?

- Snow is made from frozen, solidified water. It is cold and can feel wet to the touch.

ACTIVITY: Which is the best sort of snow?

You will need:

- magic snow/insta snow – (not edible so must be supervised) available on the internet
- baking powder
- cornflour
- glitter
- cooking oil
- water
- cotton wool
- hole puncher
- white paper
- snow flake sequins
- ice cubes
- chopping board
- rolling pin
- any other materials you can find that look like snow and are suitable for use with your class
- waterproof aprons!

Storify the science

Read the book to your class. Show them the front cover and ask them what clues there are that this is a winter story. They'll soon spot the snow. However, many young children connect snow with Christmas rather than winter so be sure to tackle this misconception. Many won't ever have seen snow so you may need to provide some virtual experience by watching video clips of snow falling and children playing in the snow. Write down all the words they use to describe what snow looks like and feels like.

Tip some snowflake sequins into your hand. Discuss with the children whether it looks like real snow. Let the children look closely at a few sequins and feel them. Check back against the words you wrote on the board. Is it sparkly? Yes! Is it cold? No! Could I make a snowman with it? No!

Reach the conclusion that the snowflake sequins are not very much like real snow. Lots of things look like snow in some way but only a few will behave like snow too. We are going to select the best material to make snow in the classroom!

 ## Set the challenge

You are going to make some different kinds of snow to play with. We'll make enough of each to fill a tray. Then we can look at the snow we made and find the one we think is the most like real snow. Remember not to put any of it in your mouth.

When you compare the types of snow, think about whether it:

- feels like real snow
- looks like real snow
- moves like real snow
- melts like real snow
- sticks together like real snow.

Once you have investigated all the kinds of snow, decide which one is the most like real snow. You must have a reason for your choice.

You could find out which is the class favourite and why.

You could ask other groups of people if they agree with you. Ask the adults in your class, ask your parents and carers, ask the adults in the office and ask the older children in your school.

You could even do a survey!

Snow recipes (all require adult supervision)

1 Gloopy snow

- 200 g cornflour
- about 150 ml water.

Mix until the gloop is like thick custard. You want to reach a point where there are no pockets of dry cornflour then stop adding water. If you make it too watery, leave it to settle and pour off the water that collects at the top.

2 Snow dough

- 200 g cornflour
- 120 ml vegetable oil
- 1 teaspoon of glitter.

Mix to a silky breadcrumb consistency.

3 Baking powder snow

- 200 g baking powder
- a little water – up to 80 ml.

Add the water really slowly until you get a breadcrumb consistency.

4 Paper snow

Use the hole-puncher to make tiny circles of white paper. You'll need to punch a lot of holes (and take care not to punch any holes in little fingers) to get enough paper snow to play with so you might want to borrow a few hole-punchers.

5 Crushed ice snow

Place the ice cubes in a strong plastic bag, seal the end and put the bag on a chopping board on a sturdy surface. Now use the rolling pin to crush the ice.

6 Magic/insta snow

Follow the instructions on the packet. One small packet makes buckets of snow so you won't need to buy more than one packet. Remember, this is not edible.

7 Other types of snow

If you have other safe materials that resemble snow that the children can handle, then include those in this activity.

Teacher's top tips

Give the children plenty of time to play and investigate the different materials. Let them make snowballs. Let them pull toy sledges (or boxes on strings) through the snow. Let them put model people in the snow to see whether they sink.

Do try to keep all the types of snow separate for as long as possible to allow the children to compare them.

Make as many types of snow as you think appropriate for your class but you'll need three at the very least.

If you choose to make the snow with the children, then you'll probably want to work in small groups. However, if you can make the different snows in advance (and have a freezer/icebox to keep the crushed ice cold) you could put a tray of each snow, ready made, on tables for the children and thus run it as a whole class activity.

Don't leave the inedible magic snow out, unsupervised, where children can eat it.

The important skills here are observing, describing, choosing the best material for the job and giving a reason for that choice.

You could also take the opportunity to introduce tally charts, pictograms or bar charts by taking a survey of people's choices.

KEY QUESTIONS to help children to move towards an understanding:

- What do you want to try?
- Can you describe this one?
- What does it feel like?
- Which one is more like snow?
- Why?
- Is there anything else like that?
- What else would you like to try?

 Finale

Find a beautiful video clip (preferably time lapse) on the internet, of snowflakes forming and watch the awe on the children's faces when they see how spectacular snowflakes are, when viewed close up.

Get out the snowflake sequins you used at the start. Notice that they are roughly the right shape for snowflakes but they are way too big and nothing else about them makes them look or feel like snow.

What next?

If you want to record your findings in a creative way then you could:

- Ages 4–5: snow is the perfect place to practise forming your letters. Try writing your name with your finger in the different kinds of snow. Try writing 'Noi' or 'whale' or 'snow'! You could even write 'best' in the best kind of snow.

- Make a class pictogram. Draw a large pair of axes. Stick a photo of each kind of snow along the bottom axis. Give the children a snowflake shaped piece of paper and let them stick it above the type of snow that seems most like real snow to them, to make a column.

- Collect information for a bar chart by asking opinions and tallying up the responses. They could write about the reasons people gave for choosing a particular type of snow.

- Make a mini-book, with a picture of a different type of snow on each page. The children can write describing words around each picture. They can show which they chose as the best snow with a big tick.

- Pretend to be Noi. Write a poem about snow that uses all the words you chose to describe it.

- Role-play being Noi, talking about the snow you made. Explain which you think is the most like real snow and why. Include all your observations about how it feels, how it moves and whether it sticks together.

Look out for evidence of scientific thinking and learning

- The children use their senses to explore the snow.
- The children make observations, e.g. this snow is colder than that one.
- The children make links, e.g. this one melts just like snow because it's made of ice, like snow.
- The children ask questions, e.g. what happens if I add more water?
- The children test ideas to find answers, e.g. I want to see whether you can make snowballs with the dry ones.
- The children can sort the materials, e.g. these two are wet and sticky but that one is dry.

EXPLORING ICE

Story link

Noi stepped onto the ice.

THE SCIENCE: Ice forms on the top of the water

Ice is water in a solid state. When water freezes, the molecules spread out a little so if you put a sealed bottle of water in the freezer, it will crack or push out the stopper as the water expands to form ice.

As ice is less dense than water, it floats. You can see this because ice floats at the top of your glass of water. (You can read more about density on p. 51 in Traction Man.)

Seawater will freeze in the same way but at a lower temperature than fresh water.

Ice that is 10 cm thick is considered safe to walk on. Any less than 5 cm and it can break easily and you can end up stuck under the ice. It is often impossible to tell how thick the ice is from above, so walking on ice is a risky thing to do. However, when ice reaches 25 cm, it may well be strong enough to support a car.

What do the children need to know?

- Ice floats on water.
- Ice forms because the water gets really cold.
- Ice needs to be very thick before you can safely stand on it so you should never walk on ice that has formed over deep water such as ponds or rivers.

INVESTIGATION: Making an ice bridge

You will need:

- cold weather!
- different shaped plastic containers, including balloons, that can be frozen
- a large freezer
- lots of ice cubes
- lots of large blocks of ice made by freezing water in different shaped containers, including balloons for spherical ice cubes

- water trays
- large water tray
- small plastic model of a boy (Noi)
- model of a lighthouse
- toy boat
- waterproof aprons and gloves.

Storify the science

Look back over the story. Stop when you reach the page where Noi steps out on to the ice. Ask the children if you think it is safe for Noi to walk on the ice.

Discuss what might happen if he went through – he'd get wet and cold, he might not be able to climb out etc. Explain that if you run onto the ice, and fall through it you would keep going forward and get stuck under the ice.

The story says Noi thought that he must be careful. Discuss how he might have been careful. Think about the shoes he wore and the way he walked.

Put out a tray of water and place the model of Noi at one edge. On the opposite edge, place a lighthouse (or torch). In the centre of the water tray, place the boat. Explain that you'd like to recreate the scene from the book where Noi walks across the ice to find his father and ends up in the lighthouse. But how can I make the ice? Noi needs thick ice to walk across in the story. How could we get the ice to make a solid layer?

 # Set the challenge

You are going to try to make a layer of ice for Noi to walk across so we can re-create that part of the story.

You might like to use some ice that is already frozen. You might like to make some ice of your own.

Think about:

- how you could make ice;
- how you could make ice in a particular shape;
- what happens to ice when you put it in water;
- how to make a flat sheet of ice that Noi could walk on.

Remember to wear waterproof clothes and gloves to keep your hands warm.

What did you try? Did your idea work?

 # Teacher's top tips

Safety first! Be aware that ice that you get straight out of a freezer may stick to fingers. Wear gloves.

You'll probably want to work in small groups as adult help is required.

The important skill here is tinkering! Scientists often have to try out an idea and then observe what happens so they can improve upon what they did and try again. This is tinkering. Children need time to explore things to observe what happens and then have time to try something else.

Keep asking:

- What happened?
- Why?
- What would you like to try next?

Try to facilitate whatever the children's ideas are. Be prepared to put trays of water in the fridge/freezer or leave trays out overnight in sub zero temperatures.

Notice that the ice always floats to the top. Any ice forming on water trays, overnight, forms at the top.

Spend time playing with the ice, investigating whether or not you can get it to stick together like when you made snowballs.

It may take time to get results so you may want to let the investigation run for a few days. These are some ideas you may want to suggest:

- Try crushing ice and floating it on cold water – can you get it to stick together to make a sheet?
- Try filling the tray with large lumps of ice – can you make a stable platform of ice?
- Try working with ice inside the classroom vs outside. What is the difference?
- Try cooling the water – can you make it into ice?

You'll probably want to run this session in your outdoor area in wellies and waterproofs and gloves!

Many children won't have a concept of how cold it must be for ice to form. This investigation will help them to realise that one ice cube in a tray of water won't cause the whole tray to freeze.

If you time it right, you'll be able to leave the tray out on a cold night and enjoy the magic moment when the children discover that the ice has formed and Noi can walk across it to the lighthouse.

If you have an outdoor thermometer, you can check the temperature, during the day, to see how cold it is. You might be able to record the temperature overnight to see how cold it was when the water froze. Failing that, the weather forecast will tell give you a rough guide to the overnight temperature. You could track the temperature with the children to show how cold it must be for ice to form.

Take lots of photos!

Note that it is usually in winter that we experience temperatures that are cold enough for ice and snow. You could look at weather forecasts with the children and note the blue colour denoting cold weather.

KEY QUESTIONS to help children to move towards an understanding:

- What do you want to try?
- How will you do it?
- What shape will it be?
- What will you use?
- Where will you put it?
- Did it turn out like you expected?
- What would you like to try next?

 # What next?

If you want to record your findings in a creative way then you could:

- Ages 4–5: make a little book to show what you tried. This could be pre-prepared with pages that read 'I tested _____ . Did it work? ____' Save the one that works for the last page!
- Role-play being an ice bridge engineer. Tell Noi how he can make an ice bridge.
- Take a photo of the ice bridge you made. Write instructions so Noi can make one.
- Write a Tinkering Log Book. Write down what you tried and what you observed.
- Write an extra page for the book where Noi tries to walk on ice that is not thick enough. Describe how he slips and tips.
- Write a new story about Noi walking on thin ice and falling into the water. Does the Storm Whale save him this time?

 # Look out for evidence of scientific thinking and learning

- The children find ways to make ice.
- The children make observations, e.g. the ice floats on the water.
- The children make links, e.g. the puddles/ice trays in the shade are still frozen.
- The children ask questions, e.g. will all the water freeze if I put some ice in it?
- The children test ideas to find answers, e.g. I wonder if the water will freeze if I take it outside.
- The children review how well their method of making ice worked.

_____

DOES EVERYTHING FREEZE?

Story link

The sea was frozen.

 THE SCIENCE: Freezing other liquids

Water is not the only liquid that can be frozen.

Salt water, like seawater can be frozen but it must be cooled to a lower temperature as the salt molecules 'get in the way' of the formation of ice crystals.

Fruit cordials and juices are mostly water so they freeze in much the same way as water. Juices containing pulp may not freeze so well as the pulp will not behave in the same way as the water.

Oils will also freeze to a solid. However, oils are made from many different molecules and each type can have a different freezing temperature so they can look quite interesting as they freeze and it is hard to specify an exact freezing point for an oil. Olive oil will begin to solidify in the fridge.

Milk is full of water so it will freeze but the exact temperature will be affected by the amount of sugar and salt and fat in the milk.

What do the children need to know?

* Other liquids can be frozen to make solids.

 INVESTIGATION: Solidifying liquids

You will need:

* transparent pots or plastic cups
* oil
* milk
* juice
* squash (cordial)
* water
* other liquids as suggested by the children

* salt
* tray of water
* block of ice
* ice pops/fruit juice ice pops (not yet frozen) – enough for one each to eat and some to test
* freezer.

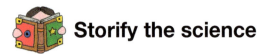

Storify the science

Put a tray of water and a block of ice out where all the children can see them.

Re-read the first few pages of the story. Notice that the sea is a liquid at the start. Show how the tray of water can be tipped to make waves like at the start of the story but the water in the block of ice doesn't move.

Return to the page where Noi is playing on the beach. Ask the children if they have ever been to the seaside. Ask them what the seawater is like. Ask if it is the same as bathwater, drinking water or even swimming pool water.

Then, turn to the page where the sea has frozen. Remind the children about the water they froze last week – it wasn't seawater. In the book, it says the seawater froze. If seawater can freeze maybe other liquids can freeze. Ask the children if they know about any other liquids that freeze. Listen to all their suggestions. They may have made ice lollies at home.

Tell the children that you are going to find out about freezing different liquids. Show them the liquids you have already gathered. Ask the children if there are any others they would like to investigate and be prepared to make them available if they are safe to use in the classroom.

Model some questions they might like to answer by telling them things you wonder about, e.g. I wonder if you can freeze oil. I wonder if you can freeze milk. I wonder if milk will freeze as quickly as water. I wonder if frozen salt water looks the same as frozen tap water. Ask the children what they wonder about. Give them time to talk to a partner. Write the ideas down.

Show the children the ice pops. Ask what you could try with them. They are likely to suggest freezing them and eating them, which would be fun to do (check for children with food allergies) but they may suggest possible tests such as I wonder if the red ones freeze faster than the yellow ones.

Set the challenge

You are going to find out about freezing liquids.

First, decide which liquids you would like to investigate.

You could:

- choose one liquid to see whether it freezes;
- choose two liquids to compare;
- think up your own idea.

Mark a line about halfway up your cup(s). Fill your cup up to the line with your chosen liquid(s).

Write down what you think might happen.

Ask your adult helper to put your cup(s) in the freezer.

When you check your cup(s) think about:

- what looks different;
- what feels different;
- whether the liquid is frozen;
- whether what you expected to happen . . . actually happened;
- what happens as your liquid melts.

What did you find out?

 # Teacher's top tips

The important skills here are generating questions, measuring accurately and observing the changes.

Questions they may ask:

- Which freezes first? (be prepared to check on them a few times over the day)
- Will this freeze?
- What happens if you freeze . . .?

The children may notice that the liquid has changed in appearance. They may also notice that it has increased in volume, expanding up and over the line they marked.

The solids may look odd as they melt so allow plenty of time to observe the solids melting again afterwards. For example, the water part of milk will freeze and may stay frozen longer than the fats and proteins so you may see an icy core in the cup.

Shop-bought ice pops will more or less freeze within a school day but larger cups of water will take overnight so check them the following day.

Often, an unexpected outcome will lead to further questions. If you can, allow time for further explorations.

Don't forget to eat the ice pops you froze and observe how they melt as you eat them (checking for allergies of course).

KEY QUESTIONS to help children to move towards an understanding:

- What do you want to try?
- How will you do it?
- What might happen?
- What did happen?
- What is the answer to your question?

What next?

If you want to record your findings in a creative way then you could:

- Ages 4–5: make your own ice pops using a fruit juice of your choice (being aware of children with allergies).

- Make a mini-book with a photo of one of the liquids you froze on each page. Write 'It froze' next to each liquid that froze to a solid.

- Make a cartoon strip to show what happened. Draw the liquid, then the frozen solid and then the stages it goes through as it thaws. Write speech bubbles for the liquids saying 'I'm frozen' or 'I've gone cloudy' to show your observations.

- Role-play being Noi and his father making ice pops. Noi could be showing his father how to make them. Talk about how the liquids change as they freeze. You could even write a recipe.

Look out for evidence of scientific thinking and learning

- The children think of their own ideas.
- The children make observations, e.g. the oil goes cloudy.
- The children make links, e.g. the salty water froze just like the seawater in the story.
- The children ask questions, e.g. does oil freeze?
- The children test ideas to find answers, e.g. I think the pink ones might freeze faster so I'm going to try pink ones and yellow ones and see which freezes first.
- The children measure out the liquid accurately.

RESCUING THE BOAT

Story link
The whale family breaks the ice.

THE SCIENCE: Investigating melting ice

Large chunks of ice will melt more slowly in water than smaller pieces. Imagine a large ice cube. The water can only touch the outside of the cube. There is a lot of ice inside the cube, which the water cannot reach. Heat is transferred from the water to the ice at the surface of the ice cube to melt it. This heat can only reach the surface of the cube.

Now imagine crushing this ice cube. Now, the water can reach the ice that was once in the middle of the cube and there are lots more little pieces with lots more surface that the heat can reach. The more surface area the ice has, the faster it will melt.

Warm water will melt ice faster than cold water because it has more heat energy to transfer to the ice.

When snow is forecast, the roads are 'gritted' with a mixture of sand and salt. But why?

When salt (sodium chloride) is dissolved in water it is broken up into sodium ions and chloride ions. These ions are present in the salty water, even though we cannot see them. When the water freezes, the molecules of water must bond back together to make their solid structure but the sodium ions and chloride ions in the salt water prevent this from happening. It is harder for salty water to freeze so it freezes at a lower temperature.

If you sprinkle salt onto an ice cube, the salt will dissolve in the thin layer of water at the surface (where the ice has melted) and make salt water. The sodium and chloride ions in the salt water can then act upon the solid ice structure, interacting with the water molecules and breaking the bonds that hold them in the solid structure so that it becomes a liquid. The ice becomes liquid salt water.

Of course, if it is cold enough, even salty water will freeze but the saltier the water, the lower the freezing point so a good sprinkle of salt on the road can make the thin layer of ice very salty and lower the freezing point enough to melt the ice.

What do the children need to know?

- You can free the boat by breaking the ice up. The smaller pieces of ice will melt faster too.
- You can melt the ice using warm water.`
- If you sprinkle salt on the ice, you will make salty water which will be a liquid at much lower temperature.

 # ACTIVITY: Ways to melt the ice

You will need:

- small plastic boats (at least one per child)
- ice cube trays or margarine tubs if the boats won't fit in ice cube trays
- large freezer
- pots of warm water (max 40 °C for safety)

- wooden spoons
- salt
- flour
- sugar
- plastic trays to catch the drips
- waterproof aprons

Storify the science

Read the part of the story where Noi finds his father's boat, frozen into the ice. Look at what the whales do to free the boat. Ask the children if they have ever broken ice. Talk about ice puddles and how you can break the ice by stamping on the ice. But the ice in the story was very thick ice. It needed a very strong whale to break it.

Show the children the little boats, frozen into the ice cubes or ice blocks.

 ## Set the challenge

You are going to help free these boats from the ice.

You can use any of the equipment we have provided.

Find as many different ways to free the boats from the ice as you can.

Which method freed the boats most quickly?

 ## Teacher's top tips

The important skills here are observing and tinkering: trying out lots of different things to see what happens. Allow as much time as you can and provide as much ice as you can.

You may find that the children set up a comparative test – racing one melting method against another. If so, you could encourage them to think about how to race them fairly.

The children may try:

- hitting the ice with the spoons – avoid damage to fingers and trays but, if you can see they are working with purpose, allow some use of the wooden spoons to crack the ice;
- pouring warm water on the ice;
- covering the ice with the flour/sugar/salt;
- making salt water to pour over the ice;
- making warm salty water to pour over the ice.

They may have ideas of their own. Wherever safe and possible, enable the children to try their ideas, even if you know they won't work. Misconceptions can be addressed in this way.

KEY QUESTIONS to help children to move towards an understanding:

- What do you want to try?
- What do you think will happen?
- Will it make a difference if . . .?
- What else do you want to try?
- Can you find a faster way?

What next?

If you want to record your findings in a creative way then you could:

- Ages 4–5: prepare in advance, a large drawing of a boat stuck in the ice. Draw the equipment you had available at the bottom of the picture with a pre-written sentence – 'I used the _____ to free the ship'. The children could circle the items they used and complete the sentence.

- Write an alternative ending to the book where Noi rescues his father's boat from the ice using a method you found was successful when you tested it.

- Role-play Noi and his father having a conversation about how to free the boat from the ice and then role-play them freeing the boat using the method they decided would work best. You could dress up and take photos of yourself. Write speech bubbles around the photos explaining what you are doing.

Look out for evidence of scientific thinking and learning

- The children make decisions about how to approach their task.
- The children make observations, e.g. the ice cube was too thick to break with the spoon.
- The children make links, e.g. they put salt on the icy path at school to make it melt.
- The children ask questions, e.g. would it be really quick with hot water?
- The children test ideas to find answers, e.g. I'm going to try putting sugar on the ice to see what happens.
- The children test ideas in a comparative test, e.g. I'm going to race the cold water and the warm water to see which is first.
- The children can sort the materials, e.g. the flour and the sugar didn't make the ice melt but the salt did.

_____

6   *The Tiny Seed*

Eric Carle (1970)

TOPIC PLANNER

Story link	Science: Growing plants	Activity	Page
The seed	Classification	Seed sorting (activity)	93–4
The wind	Seeds dispersed by the wind Predicting and testing Recording in a table	Investigating materials that can be blown by the wind (investigation)	97
Landing	Planting seeds Predicting and testing	Investigating planting in: • cold • salty water • hot and dry • damp soil • children's ideas (investigation)	103
Germinating	Germination – absorbing water Observing	Swelling up Insta-snow and plastic beads/cubes Soaking bean seeds (activity)	108
Broken	Capillary action Observing	Transporting water upwards Using capillary action to make water travel upwards (extension activity 6+)	111–12
Growing taller	Photosynthesis Observing Naming plants	Can it grow without leaves? Naming plants by their leaves (activity)	116

Story link	Science:	Activity	Page
Think like a bee	Flowers and plant life cycles Observing Naming animals	Sensing flowers Teaching the bees (activity)	120–1

N.B. You may not be able to do all these activities with children with allergies. Check first!

THE SEED

Story link
One of the seeds is smaller than all the others

THE SCIENCE: Classification (grouping organisms by their features)

Linnaeus (1707–78) was a Swedish botanist who was determined to find a way to systematically name plants so that plants with similar features could be grouped together. He improved upon the ideas of other botanists who came before him and grouped and named all the plants and animals that had been identified at the time, according to his binomial (two name – genus/species) system. He used the physical features of the plants and animals (e.g. number of stamens or seed type) to put them into sensible groups.

Classification helps scientists to organise the huge array of living things into groups. Once organised, the differences between different species or different groups are easier to observe.

When grouping living things, we need to look closely at important features that distinguish one animal from another. Choosing which feature to focus upon is important. Both a moth and a cheetah can be spotty but this doesn't put the two animals into the same group. The warm blood of the cheetah and its four legs distinguish it from the cold blooded, six legged moth.

When considering seeds, there are various key things to look for, namely:

- size
- colour
- shape

- texture of the surface
- the fruit or pod it came from.

Young children often choose groupings that are illogical, e.g. spotty/round/fuzzy. They need to know that groupings have to answer **one** question at a time, e.g. 'What colour is it?' Red/brown black *or* 'Does it float?' Yes/No.

What do the children need to know?

- Seeds are found in all kinds of structures such as fruits, pods and fir cones.
- If you plant a seed and look after it, it will grow into a plant that looks like the one it came from.
- We can group plants and seeds according to what they look like.

 ## ACTIVITY: Seed sorting

You will need:

- fruits including oranges, strawberries, apples and peaches (avoid seedless varieties!)
- pine cone
- bean or pea pod
- dandelion clock
- a mixture of different seeds including bird seed (without meal worms or nuts if children have allergies) dried runner bean seeds, dried peas, cress seeds and any other interesting seeds you can get hold of
- trays
- tweezers
- small pots of water.

 ## Storify the science

Read the whole story of *The Tiny Seed* to the children. Ask them to tell you what happened in the story. Ask them which seed grew into the biggest plant. Elicit that the smallest seed grew into the biggest flower. Ask the children how being small helped the flower – it wasn't seen by the bird and the mouse etc.

Ask the children to name any seeds they know of. If they are stumped by this question, ask them if they've ever eaten beans or peas and explain that these are seeds. They may also have experience of seeds in muesli. And of course, nuts are seeds too. They may mention seeds that are inside fruits. Have the fruits to hand and as they are mentioned, show them to the children and ask them where the seeds are.

Spend a little time opening up each fruit, pod or cone to reveal the very different seeds. Blow the dandelion clock so that the children can look at a seed each.

If you have a hand held magnifier, use it to project a close-up image of the seed onto the board so the children can observe it closely.

Brainstorm words to describe each seed until you have a bank of terms that include colours, textures, patterns, sizes and whether it rolls or not.

 # Set the challenge

You are going to sort out this mixture of seeds. Sort the seeds into groups and give each group a name, e.g. Red seeds.

You will be asked to do this activity a few times.

 # Teacher's top tips

The point of this activity is to help the children, by trial and error, to learn to sort objects into sensible groups based on one feature alone, e.g. colour OR pattern. Let the children sort the objects and then share their groups with you. Find children who have chosen sensible groupings based on one feature and explain why those make sense.

Listen out for the following errors:

- nonsensical grouping, e.g. red seeds/flat seeds/ spotty seeds. This grouping involves both colour and form;
- groupings that are subjective and hence won't be agreed upon by all, e.g. nice seeds and horrible seeds.

Gently encourage them to stick to one obvious visible physical feature at a time, instead.

Repeat the process a few times to make sure every child can accurately group the objects according to physical features. You might want to swap trays of seeds and have slightly different mixes in each tray to keep the level of challenge up.

The important skills here are observation and sensible sorting. If you listen to the chatter as the groups sort the seeds you'll hear plenty of observations and justifications as to why a seed should or shouldn't go in a particular group.

When you are on the last round, you may like to introduce floating and sinking as a way of sorting by giving them a pot of water to try the seeds in. Avoid using water until the end as the seeds won't roll when wet and sticky.

KEY QUESTIONS to help children to move towards an understanding:

- What do you notice about these?
- Are they all like that?
- Can you find ones that are the same in some way?
- Can you describe this one?
- Where will you put it?
- Do these belong together?
- Why?

What next?

If you want to record your findings in a creative way then you could:

- Ages 4–5: match photographs of the fruits with the photographs of the seeds that came out of them.
- Choose a question about the seeds. Write that question at the top of the page, e.g. Is the seed red? And under the question, glue the seeds to the page in two groups – yes or no.
- Role-play being Jack from 'Jack and the Beanstalk'. Describe your bean seeds from the magic beanstalk. Draw a big picture of it and write words to describe its size, shape and texture all around it.
- Make a mini book of fruits. Draw each fruit cut open with the seed clearly showing inside. Write a descriptive sentence about each seed at the bottom of the page.
- Make a collage of a giant seed. Choose fabrics and materials that have the right texture or pattern to match your seed.

Look out for evidence of scientific thinking and learning

- The children use their senses to explore the seeds.
- The children make observations, e.g. the seeds are on the outside of the strawberry.
- The children make links, e.g. lots of the seeds are very small.
- The children ask questions, e.g. is it heavier than the others?
- The children can sort the seeds into sensible groups.

_____

THE WIND

Story link

The autumn wind blew the tiny seed.

THE SCIENCE: Seeds that are dispersed by the wind

Two plants growing near each other will compete with one another for water and light. An established plant with longer roots and leaves growing higher up on the stalk is more likely to win the competition and thrive at the expense of the smaller plant. For this reason, a species of plant that manages to get its seeds to germinate far from the parent plant will fare better.

Plants launch their seeds in various ways to get them as far from the parent plant as possible. Some have fluffy parachutes to catch the wind in passing currents of air, some have wings to help them stay in the air by spiralling down, some explode or shake their seeds out, others float in water and are carried downstream.

In this story, the seed is blown by the wind but it has no parachute or wings. It would need to be quite light for it to catch the wind.

What do the children need to know?

- Seeds must grow in a space away from the parent plant.
- Only very light seeds will be carried on the wind in this way.

INVESTIGATION: Investigating materials that can be blown by the wind

You will need:

- drinking straws
- foil
- marbles
- plastic cubes and other small objects that are too large to be sucked up a straw (thus avoiding choking)

- modelling clay
- wooden beads that will roll
- plastic beads that will roll
- cotton wool.

Storify the science

Revisit the page the first page of the story. The wind is blowing all the seeds along.

Ask a child to come up to the front to play the part of the seed. Tell them you are going to be the wind and then use a straw to blow at the child.

Ask the other children whether the child standing at the front has moved. Elicit that they haven't because the child is too big for you to move.

Ask the children what objects they think you could move by blowing them with the straw. Give them time to talk about this with a partner. Accept all reasonable answers.

Next, sit them around the tables, with a drinking straw each, facing each other. Put one of each of the objects listed below in the centre of each table and give them 30 seconds to discover which is easy to move around by blowing:

- a marble
- a rolled up ball of foil
- a ball of modelling clay.

Ask them to decide which is easiest to blow across the table with the straw.

Discuss their ideas. Elicit that the foil was light and it rolled and it didn't stick to the table so it was easiest to blow. With very young children you might want to give more time to exploring which objects they can move by blowing. Give them more objects (nothing small enough to suck up the straw) and more time to explore.

Now, give the children a tray of objects to look at. Include:

- some that will roll but are heavy (e.g. large wooden beads);
- some that are light but won't roll (e.g. plastic cubes);
- some that are heavy and won't roll (e.g. keys or spoons);
- some that are light and will roll well (e.g. scrunched up paper balls or cotton wool balls).

Provide the children with a pre-drawn table in which they can record their results. It might look like this:

Name of object	Prediction *I think it will move easily* ✓ ✗	Result *It moved easily* ✓ ✗
Ping pong ball	✓	✓

Set the challenge

Look at the objects in the tray. Which ones do you think would be easy to move by blowing them with a straw? Record your predictions with a tick on a table:

You'll need to decide what counts as easy to move and come up with some rules so that each object is tested fairly. The rule might be:

It counts as easy to move if I can blow it off the table with one puff from a starting line.

When you plan your test, think about:

- where the object should start;
- where your straw should be;
- how hard you will blow;
- how to make the test fair (for younger children you might ask them not to 'cheat' by tipping the table or giving it a push).

Now you can find out which objects will be easy to blow with the straw.

Test each object. Remember to record what happens with a tick in the table.

Think about what happened. Tell an adult what you found out.

Teacher's top tips

The important skills here are predicting, testing and thereby sorting the objects. Encourage them to test as fairly as they are able.

With more advanced children you may choose to ask them to draw their own table but for most of this age group a pre-drawn table for them to fill in will be challenging enough.

In order to make sensible predictions, the children need some experience of the science first. For this reason, let them experience the marble vs foil ball vs clay ball before you ask them to predict what the other materials will do, as described above. The younger/less experienced they are, the more they will need time to play and explore.

The objects will go flying so avoid sharp and pointy things.

Younger children may not be skilled at blowing rather than sucking so make sure the objects cannot be inhaled up the straw.

You may want to face all the children in one direction when they are testing the objects so that they don't blow heavier objects towards one another. Alternatively, push the table up close to a wall and have them blow towards the wall.

KEY QUESTIONS to help children to move towards an understanding:

- What do you want to try?
- Why did you choose that?
- Can you describe this object?
- What does it do when you blow it?
- Do they all do that?
- What else would you like to try?
- Is it the same or different?
- Why?

 Finale

Let the children play a game of Battle of the Winds.

- In groups of four, the children use a ping pong ball as a giant seed and straws to play a game. Defending opposite ends of a table, two children must represent the East Wind and two players must represent the West Wind.

- They must blow the ball over the end of the table (using their straws), which is defended by the opposite team (by blowing with their straws), to score a point. If it goes over the sides of the table then it gets put back in the centre to restart.

- Play to find out which way the ping pong ball seed will be blown. Will it end up in the east or the west? Whoever has the most points is the winning wind!

Lastly (taking care with children who have allergies), go outside and look for seeds being blown by the wind. Blow dandelion clocks, if you can find them. If you haven't got useful outdoor space then collect up as many seeds as you can beforehand and show them to the children now. It can be fun to look at them under a hand held digital microscope to see all the details. If it's the wrong time of year, buy seeds or birdseed to observe (avoiding the ones containing nuts). Launch seeds off the table by blowing (adults only to avoid inhaling seeds and choking). Observe how far they go.

Return to the book

Look again at the page where the seed is being blown by the wind. Ask the children to imagine how small that tiny seed must have been to be blown up high in the sky like that.

What next?

If you want to record your findings in a creative way then you could:

- Ages 4–5: sort the objects into groups according to how hard they were to move by blowing. Write a label for each group.

- Watch a dandelion clock being blown. Create a dance to show the movement.

- Make a book with a few pages. On each page prepare the beginning of a sentence so that the children can add their own word. It might read, 'The wind blew the seed over the . . .' and the children can add hills/trees/mountains etc.

- Write a letter from the seed back to the parent plant explaining how you ended up so far away.

- Draw pictures of seeds that you can see floating on the wind in your garden area. Write a sentence underneath to describe how they are travelling.

- Imagine you are the seed flying high. How would it feel? What would you see? Where do you think you would land? Write about the day you had flying in the wind.

Look out for evidence of scientific thinking and learning

- The children use their senses to explore the objects.

- The children make observations, e.g. the foil ball is much easier to move.

- The children make predictions, e.g. I think the foil ball will be easiest to move because it feels lightest.

- The children make links, e.g. the lighter objects are easier to move.

- The children ask questions, e.g. would the foil ball go up in the air?

- The children test ideas to find answers, e.g. I'm going to try blowing the ball off the edge to see if it goes up.

- The children can sort the objects, e.g. these objects are sticky and hard to move.

_____

LANDING

Story link

One seed lands on a mountain, another in the sea and another in the desert.

THE SCIENCE: Planting seeds

Seeds will germinate when they are in the right conditions. Germinating in a place that does not meet the requirements to sustain life will lead to disaster and the plant is likely to die. Each plant has specific needs in order to grow so different seeds will germinate in different conditions but the usual requirements are soil, water and warmth.

There is enough food stored within the seed for the plant to begin growing. Once the shoot has grown upwards and reached the light, it will grow a leaf and then the leaf can use the energy in sunlight to produce its own food from carbon dioxide in the air and water.

What do the children need to know?

- Plants need water, soil and warmth in order to start growing. This helps them to start growing in a good place where the adult plant will thrive.

INVESTIGATION: Investigating planting

You will need:

- seeds which grow quickly (cress and mustard or peas and runner beans)
- access to a fridge or freezer
- small plastic flower pots
- soil
- sand
- water
- salt
- a sense of adventure and a willingness to try the children's ideas no matter how whacky! You may need other equipment here that I cannot predict such as paint, lemonade, old boots, metal trays to represent wheelbarrows etc.
- film clips set in snowy and desert conditions.

Storify the science

Read the pages where the seeds begin to land. One lands on an icy mountain top. One lands in the sea. One lands in the desert. The tiny seed lands in the earth and goes to sleep.

Linger on the page with the icy mountain top. Ask the children what they think will happen. Look for evidence that plants can grow on the mountain. Think about cold winters here and snowy days – do we see flowers growing on cold snowy days? Younger children may have never seen snow but they are often familiar with films so a video clip from a film set in the snow might help them to imagine how cold it is.

Ask the children whether they can think of an icy place to grow a seed. Elicit that they could try putting seeds in the freezer.

Draw a picture of a snowy mountain top. As a group, make a prediction about what will happen to the seeds on the drawing of the mountain.

Turn to the page where a seed falls into the ocean.

Ask the children how this could be replicated in the classroom (salty water) and what they think will happen. Look for evidence that plants can grow in the sea. Note that seaweed is a plant and it grows in the sea but the tiny seed will grow into a flower so it might be different.

Once again, draw the sea and record a prediction about what might happen to the seed.

Turn to the page where a seed falls in the desert. Ask the children what they know about deserts. You could show a video clip of a desert scene from a familiar film. Ask how we could replicate this in the classroom (pot of sand in a warm dry place).

Again, draw the desert and record a prediction about what might happen to the seed.

Lastly, look at the tiny seed that fell into soil and went to sleep. Elicit that this could be replicated in soil.

Again, draw the soil and record a prediction.

Ask the children where else the seed might have landed. Give them time to talk to a partner and come up with lots of ideas. Try to facilitate testing these in some way. It might have fallen in a pot of paint, a glass of lemonade, a wheelbarrow, a rabbit run, a puddle etc. Try to follow their ideas wherever possible by providing conditions that replicate their idea, e.g. a metal tray for a wheelbarrow.

 ## Set the challenge

You are going to plant seeds in all the places that a tiny seed might land.

Wherever you plant your seed you must think about what might happen to the seed and whether it will start to grow and write down a prediction.

Try to make wise predictions based on something you have seen before or something you already know.

Make sure you label all the pots you use and remember to come back each day to see what has happened. In a week or so, we can check our seeds to see if all our predictions were right.

Return to the book

Leave the seeds long enough to see that the seeds in damp soil have sprouted. Return to the story and look through the pages. It said the snowy one could not grow – look at the one in the freezer. Check what happened and note if the prediction they recorded was right.

Repeat for the salty water, the dry sand and the damp soil, checking each one against what it said in the story and against their predictions.

Check all the other ones they planted in weird and wonderful places – note what happened and compare with the predictions.

 # Teacher's top tips

The important skills here are making predictions and testing them out. Encourage the children to think about where the seed might fall and then find a way to replicate this. Children will engage more readily if the idea is their own.

Cress and mustard seeds grow fast but are tiny and hard to handle. Peas and beans are larger and easy to manipulate but grow more slowly.

If your children are likely to put the seeds in their mouths, do check that the seeds you are using are edible. Also check for allergies – some children can be allergic to peas.

Do try out lots of different ideas but make sure someone does the four mentioned in the story, i.e. freezer, salty water, dry sand, damp soil.

Results you might see:

- Frozen seeds will look much the same.
- Seeds in paints and other chemicals are unlikely to grow.
- Salt can actually help some seeds to germinate more quickly. In some countries, the top layer of soil is salty so roots have to grow down quickly to reach fresh water.
- Seeds that remain under water are likely to go mouldy.
- Seeds grown in sweet liquids may start to sprout but if submerged will go mouldy quite fast and fresh fruit juices and milk will go off within hours so avoid using these or keep out of reach of children.
- Seeds won't germinate if kept dry.
- Seeds in well-drained soil should sprout.

Plant a few in soil yourself so you can pull a couple up to look at the roots and shoots, without causing upset by uprooting a child's plant, the following week.

KEY QUESTIONS to help children to move towards an understanding:

- What do you want to try?
- How could we do that in the classroom?

- Why did you choose that?
- What do you think will happen?
- What will it look like?
- Why?
- Where shall we put it?

What next?

If you want to record your findings in a creative way then you could:

- Ages 4–5: take a photo of yourself next to the place you planted the seed. If it grew – smile. If not – make a sad face.
- Write a page to go in a class book of the Tiny seed. Instead of the snowy mountain or the sea, write a new paragraph about one of the other places it landed and what happened, e.g. 'One seed tumbles into a wellington boot. It is dark and dry and there is no soil inside. The seed cannot grow. But the tiny seed flies on.' Illustrate it with paint effects and collage in the style of Eric Carle.
- Make a mini-book with one of the places you planted seeds drawn and labelled on each page. Under each place, write whether or not the seed could grow there.
- Draw a map of all the places the seed flies over before it lands in the soil. With younger children, you could retell this bit of the story by re-enacting the seed travelling around the map. With older children, you could label each place and write instructions for the seed about where to land and why.
- Make a snakes and ladders type game where the tiny seed is the counter. If it lands on damp soil, it can go up the ladder towards the end. And if it lands on an icy mountain or hot dry desert or salty sea it must go backward down a snake.

Look out for evidence of scientific thinking and learning

- The children have their own ideas about where to plant the seeds.
- The children make observations, e.g. the flowers in my garden don't grow in the winter.
- The children make predictions, e.g. I don't think it will grow in the sand as there aren't any flowers in the sandpit.
- The children make links, e.g. If it won't grow in the ice it won't grow in the freezer.
- The children ask questions, e.g. Will my seed start to grow in lemonade?
- The children test ideas to find answers, e.g. I'm going to try planting my seed in lemonade to see whether it grows.

_____

GERMINATING

Story link

It is spring and the seed starts to grow.

THE SCIENCE: Germination

In order for the seed to germinate, the outer coating (the seed coat) must break open. Before it germinates, this coat is tough and hard to keep the contents of the seed safe. The first stage of germination is, therefore, to soften this seed coat.

When the seed is soaked by the rain, it absorbs water which both softens the seed coat and makes the inside of the seed swell up so that it splits the seed coat apart, allowing the first root and first shoot to grow out of the seed.

What do the children need to know?

- Seeds need to be wet in order to start growing.
- The seeds soak up water and swell up and then the seed coat splits.

ACTIVITY: Swelling up

You will need:

- insta snow – instant snow powder
- plastic beads or cubes (suitable for the children to handle)
- coloured plastic plates
- basil seeds or chia seeds
- runner bean seeds
- other types of seed that have been dried and are safe to use with children
- pots
- water
- magnifying glasses
- hand held magnifier
- germinated bean seed from last activity
- bean seed soaked for a couple of days in water.

Storify the science

Today, start with this activity rather than the book. It's going to get messy so prepare the room. Give the children a plate with a teaspoonful of the instant snow powder on it (one between two). This is not edible so don't leave children unattended.

On another plate, put a spoonful of beads or cubes.

Allow the children to touch the powder and the beads/cubes and tell you how they feel.

Now ask them to pour a little water from a suitable pot onto each plate. It doesn't really matter how much they add, but encourage them to add a little to begin with as the insta snow looks most like snow at the start. (As you add more it gets slushy.) Enjoy the reaction as the children see the powder swell before their eyes. When they add water to the flour beads/cubes there will be no change – they won't swell up.

Ask them what they think has happened. Encourage them to tell you all their ideas and listen out for anything that shows an understanding that the water has been soaked up by the insta-snow powder but not by the beads/cubes. Introduce the word 'absorb'. Talk about things that absorb water. Ask the children if everything absorbs water. Think about the beads/cubes, the pot and the plate.

Wash hands!

Now, return to the book. Read the page where spring arrives and the seeds burst open. Focus on that line. Ask the children what they think that means. Look closely at the pictures. You can see the roots and the shoots coming out of the seed.

If you have one left from last week, show them a germinating bean seed with the root and shoot emerging from the seed.

Ask the children how they think it burst open.

 ## Set the challenge

You are going to find out more about what happens when seeds get wet.

- Choose some seeds to investigate.
- Put some of each type in warm water and keep some of each type of seed dry so you can compare them later.
- Leave the seeds on the table and keep an eye on them.
- Do the dry seeds change?
- Do the wet seeds change?
- In what way do the seeds change?
- Draw or photograph the wet and dry seeds to compare them.
- Talk about what you have observed.

 # Finale

Use the hand held digital microscope to project an image of the seeds onto the whiteboard. Show them a dry bean seed compared to one that has been soaking for a day. Talk about the fact that it has swelled up because it has absorbed the water, just like the instant snow powder.

If the seed coat has split, try sliding the coat off. Look again at the sprouted bean and the pictures you looked at earlier. Remind the children that the seeds have a coat to protect them but the roots and shoots have to get out and the water softens the coat and makes the inside swell so the coat will split to let the root and shoot out.

 # Teacher's top tips

The important skill here is observation so allow plenty of time. It may take 20 minutes for the seeds and beans to absorb the water and fully swell up so you may want to set it up and then go out to play and look for changes afterwards.

The snow doesn't show up well on white plates so use coloured ones if you can. A coloured piece of paper on the plate works too.

You should get a satisfying reaction from the children as they watch the chia and basil seeds soaking in water, because these seeds will visibly swell, producing a layer of 'jelly' around them, that looks like frogspawn. You can see that the outer layer of the seed has swollen up by absorbing water. (This jelly like layer is thought to help the rest of the seed hydrate and stay hydrated.) Likewise, the beans will swell up as the water is absorbed. You won't notice the difference in the runner bean seeds unless you have a dry one to compare it to but they do swell up as the water is absorbed and will eventually split, although this might take longer, so have one soaking for a day or two before this lesson. Seeds will swell up noticeably faster in water that is a little warmer than water from the cold tap.

KEY QUESTIONS to help children to move towards an understanding:

- What do you notice about these?
- Are they all like that?
- Do they all do the same thing?
- Can you find ones that are the same some way?
- Can you describe this one?
- What does it look like under the magnifying glass?
- Has something happened?
- Why do you think that is?

What next?

If you want to record your findings in a creative way then you could:

- Ages 4–5: put chia seeds or sweet basil seeds in the water tray and explore the frog-spawn texture.

- Draw careful pictures or take photos of the seeds before and after soaking. Write labels for each and write about the changes you saw happen.

- Role-play being a gardener on the TV or radio and explain how to germinate your seeds by soaking them and then plant them in soil in a warm spot so they can start growing. You could write these instructions down.

Look out for evidence of scientific thinking and learning

- The children observe and explore the seeds.
- The children notice when the seeds swell up and get bigger.
- The children make observations, e.g. there's jelly around the seed.
- The children make links, e.g. some materials soak up water.
- The children ask questions, e.g. what happens if you put peas in water?

BROKEN

Story link
A child steps on a plant and breaks it so it cannot grow anymore.

THE SCIENCE: Capillary action

Inside the stem of a plant, there are tiny tubes that carry the water up the plant and carry the food (sugar) made in the leaves to the rest of the plant.

The water starts in the soil but is absorbed by the roots and ends up at the top of the plant. This can be a long way up, if the tree is tall. It is hard to move water upwards as you are moving the water against the force of gravity. The process by which plants achieve this is called capillary action.

This is how capillary action works. The tubes inside the plant stem are very tiny. When water enters the tubes it is attracted to the walls of the tubes so it creeps up the edges of the tubes. The molecules in water are also attracted to each other so as the water creeps up the sides of the tubes the front molecules pull more molecules along behind. This would be impossible in a wide tube because there would be a wide and heavy column of water to pull up. It only works this way because the tubes are tiny so the amount of water being dragged up each tube is tiny too.

If the stem is damaged, the tubes inside may be blocked or disconnected and the flow of water and sugars is interrupted. Worse still, bacteria and fungal spores can enter the plant if the stem is broken and will grow well in this food rich and moist environment. These infections can end up killing the plant.

Paper is made from wood fibres.

If you put cheap kitchen towel (a very absorbent paper) into water, the water soaks into the paper and is pulled up the paper by capillary action in the same way as the plant. You can see the water move upwards, above the water line.

What do the children need to know?

* Water is absorbed upwards by kitchen towel. The water is moving through tiny tubes and tiny spaces in the kitchen towel.
* Water moves up the plant from the roots to the stem through tiny tubes and spaces.

 EXTENSION ACTIVITY: Transporting water upwards (for ages 6+)

You will need:

* a short straw (cut a longer one in half)
* drinking straws
* art straws
* clean plastic tubing (at least 1 cm wide) – clean for drinking through
* large clean tub of clean water (coloured with food colouring)
* step ladder/safe high place to stand
* cut flowers
* hand held digital microscope
* kitchen towel (the cheaper ones work better)
* pots of coloured water
* empty pots
* glittery water, lemonade and other liquids
* different types of paper
* freezer bag clips.

 Storify the science

Start outside, next to the tallest tree or plant you can find. Bring your stepladders next to the plant or place them nearby, ready to use. (You may need a risk assessment to use stepladders.)

Pick a leaf and squash it with your fingers. Show the children that your fingers are now wet. (You could press the leaf inside a tissue to make the sap easier to see.) Ask them where that water came from. Elicit that there is water in the tree/plant. Talk about how the water gets into the plant by asking the children which part of the plant we water. We don't water the leaves – we water the roots underground. The plant takes in the water using the roots. But the water gets all the way to the top of the tree. But how?

Imagine having to suck up the water!

Place the large tub of clean coloured water at the bottom of the stepladders and climb up. Declare that you are a tall tree and put your arms out like branches. Ask the children how you could get the water from the tub up to your leaves.

Listen to all their solutions but dwell on the ideas that involve sucking up the water through a straw. Make the point that it would have to be a very long straw. Produce the short straw, then longer straws and finally the long piece of tubing. Make a big show of how hard it is to suck the water up the tubing.

Conclude that as plants don't have mouths to suck the water up, something else must be going on.

Revisit the page where the boy treads on a plant and breaks it. Ask the children which part of the plant might be broken. Use all the proper terms for the parts of the plant. Have a cut flower to hand and once they mention the stalk, snap it as you talk. The story says the broken plant cannot grow anymore.

Ask the children why they think having a broken stalk might stop the plant from growing. Elicit that the stalk carries the water up the plant – maybe the tube is broken or blocked.

 ## Set the challenge

You are going to find out why stalks are important to the plant.

You will be given some kitchen towel. Roll your kitchen towel up so that it makes a sausage shape. Put one end of the kitchen towel roll into a pot of coloured water. Hook the other end over and tuck it into an empty pot.

Look carefully. Can you see anything happening?

Leave it somewhere safe for 10 minutes. Then come back and see what has happened.

You can keep coming back to check on it all day.

Now that you've seen this, is there anything else you'd like to try?

Can you think of a way to block the flow of water so it cannot get into the other pot?

Can you think of a different material that might work like the paper?

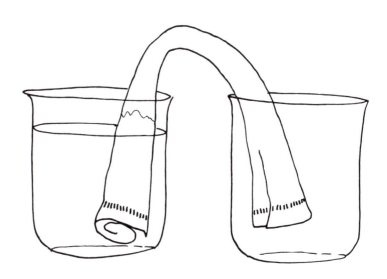

Teacher's top tips

The important skill here is observation, so give them time to observe and plenty of reminders to come back and check on their equipment.

The coloured water makes the process much easier to see.

It will take about an hour for the water to soak up through one sheet of rolled up kitchen towel. After a couple of hours, you should see water dripping into the other pot.

Try to follow the children's line of interest wherever possible and help them to set up any variation on this experiment as long as it is safe. Even if you can see it won't work, treat their idea with great interest and let them discover what happens for themselves.

You could suggest other things to test out if they don't come up with their own ideas:

- Try putting the empty pot higher up than the water pot – can you get the water to go even further uphill?
- Try different liquids – do they all move up the paper?
- Try putting glitter in the liquid – does the glitter move up the kitchen towel too?
- Try different papers – does all paper absorb as well as kitchen towel?
- Will it work with other materials?
- Try making a broken stem – tear some of the kitchen towel halfway along – does the water still move into the other pot?
- Try blocking the paper with a plastic freezer clip.

If you want to clearly see the water moving up the paper then use a hand held digital microscope to watch a droplet of water being absorbed into the kitchen towel. I find it easier to focus on the droplet and slide the paper in to meet it as, at this magnification, it absorbs really fast.

KEY QUESTIONS to help children to move towards an understanding:

- What can you see?
- What is happening?
- Can you describe it to me?
- What is happening now?
- How could we block it?

- What would you like to try?
- Have you got any questions?
- Will the glitter go up the paper too?
- Could we get it to go further? How?

 # Finale

At the end of the day you could try this:

Make three differently coloured waters. Put them in clear pots, in a row, somewhere where all the children can see them. Place two empty pots in between as shown below. Roll up kitchen towel into a sausage shape, as before, and connect up all the pots with the kitchen towel.

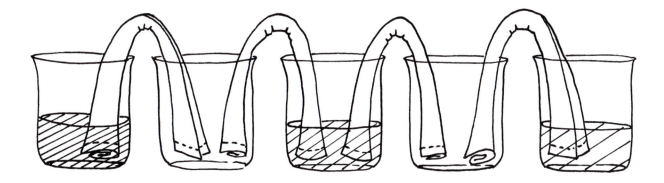

Predict, with the children, what will happen. Then, leave the pots overnight. The water will travel up the kitchen towel and the colours will end up mixing. When you come back in the morning, you should find the yellow and red have made orange, etc.

Discuss what happened!

 # What next?

If you want to record your findings in a creative way then you could:

- Take a photo of your equipment. Mark the places on the photo where there was water and label them.
- Sort materials into two piles – those that absorb water up above the water line and those that don't.
- Role-play being a scientist explaining the observations you made about water soaking up the paper. You could draw a diagram of your equipment and write instructions about how to set it up and explain the results you saw.
- Role-play being an inventor. Invent plant protectors to look after plants so that the stems don't get broken. Explain why it is important not to break the stem.

 # Look out for evidence of scientific thinking and learning

- The children make observations, e.g. the water is going up the kitchen towel.
- The children make links, e.g. if it works with water will it work with lemonade?
- The children ask questions, e.g. will the glitter end up in the other pot?
- The children test ideas to find answers, e.g. I'm going to try using this paper to see whether it works like the kitchen towel.
- The children can sort the materials into those that absorb water well and those that don't.

GROWING TALLER

Story link

The summer comes and the plant grows.

THE SCIENCE: Photosynthesis

Plants have an extraordinary ability. They can make their own food using only the energy of the sun and water and carbon dioxide. We rely on the food made by plants for our survival.

The process by which plants make their food is called photosynthesis. The energy from the sunlight is stored in the green pigment (chlorophyll) in leaves and is used to join water molecules to carbon molecules (from the carbon dioxide) to make carbohydrates (sugars).

The leaves act like little solar-panel-powered sugar factories.

These carbohydrates (sugars) are then transported to the rest of the plant so that they can be used for growth.

Generally, without leaves, the plant cannot grow.

All plants have leaves with green pigment as they need it for photosynthesis. They may not look green as they can have other coloured pigments in them too.

These leaves are different shapes depending on the type of plant and where it lives.

What do the children need to know?

*   The plant uses water, air and sunlight to make its own food in the leaves. THIS IS AMAZING!

ACTIVITY: Can it grow without leaves?

You will need:

*   two identical pot plants (which are flowering) that are not toxic. Geraniums are good. You can find advice about which plants are suitable for use in the classroom on the internet
*   leaf identification charts that include the plants in your outside area (The Woodland Trust have good online selection)
*   access to an outside area with plants in leaf
*   magnifying glasses

- hand held digital microscope
- carrot tops, grasses, pine needles and cactus spines (and other less obvious leaves).

Storify the science

Read the page about the summertime, where the plant grows and grows. Note that it also rains in summer and that when it is dry we water the plants to keep them alive.

The story says that the plant has many leaves. Count the leaves on the plant. Look how big the leaves are.

Tell the children we are going to find out why leaves are important.

Get your two identical pot plants. Leave one on the side. Take the other and begin to pull off the leaves. The children may well react and tell you not to. Ask them why you shouldn't pull off the leaves and begin discussing what the children know about leaves. (If your children are very young, employ a naughty teddy character to pull off the leaves and scold him well, thus avoiding encouraging them to do the same at home).

Do make the point that it isn't good for plants to have their leaves pulled off but you are going to do it this once so that you can study it. Leave the flowers but remove all the leaves. Place both of the plants on the windowsill in a sunny place and arrange to have them watered regularly.

Discuss with the children what they think they might see next week. Encourage them to be specific – e.g. new leaves will grow. Write all their predictions down and display their ideas next to the two plants. Ask the children to let you know what happens to the plants.

Now, pick up the leaves you pulled off the plants and give them out to the children. Look closely at them using magnifying glasses. Start noting down any features you can see, e.g. hairs, serrated edges, lobes etc.

Show the children a leaf identification chart and see if you can match up the leaf to a shape on the chart – look for similarities and differences. The pot plant probably won't be a local variety and won't be on your leaf chart but you're bound to find some similarities with other leaves.

Set the challenge

You are going to take this leaf chart outside and find as many different leaves as you can. Remember to only take one leaf from each plant.

You might be able to name the tree or the plant from the leaf. If you can't name the leaf then look carefully at the shape so you can tell me something about it.

Use your eyes to check the colour and the shape and the patterns.

Use the magnifier to look closely for hairs or little details.

Use your fingers to feel the thickness and the texture.

Keep all your leaves in a tray and practise naming them. We'll need these for a game later.

Teacher's top tips

The important skills here are close observation and naming the leaves.

There are specific words you may like to use with the children, e.g.

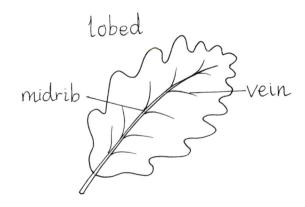

- lobed
- oval
- serrated or toothed
- palmate
- midrib
- vein.

Once you have identified some key species for your area, put up reminders in the classroom so you can keep referring back to those tree names and what their leaves look like. You may want to choose a tree to track throughout the year. The book ends with a page on autumn so you could even return to the book the next season, if you still have the same children.

You might want to laminate the leaves the children find and thus make your own leaf identification charts which could be left in the classroom for use in independent work.

There are some good leaf identification apps available for tablets, if you have them in the classroom. They may only operate when within reach of the Wi-Fi router.

KEY QUESTIONS to help children to move towards an understanding:

- What do you notice about these?
- What can you feel?
- What can you see with the magnifying glass?
- Are they all like that?

- Can you find ones that are the same in some way?
- Can you describe this one?
- Do these belong together?
- Why?

 ## Finale

Once you have spent time learning some names of your local trees and plants, bring your leaf collections inside. Ask the children to create a pile of leaves each. In pairs, they play 'snap' with the leaves. You can decide the exact rules with your group but the basic idea is that you can say snap, and win your opponent's leaves; if you can, name a way in which they are the same, e.g. SNAP – they've both got serrated edges.

You may want to ban some attributes, e.g. SNAP – they're both green.

The aim is to get the children observing the leaves and using the vocabulary to describe them. You'll overhear some fantastic debates about the leaves when they disagree.

Next week, remember to return to the pot plants and look for evidence that the plant needs leaves. It may look wilted or brown as it dies. Explain that the leaves are important, as that is where the food is made and that the leaves must be in the sunlight to make the food.

Take time to wonder about what would happen if there were no leaves.

Look back at the page in the story where it was springtime and the seed began to grow. Explain that there is a little bit of food in the seed so the plant can start to grow in the dark, under the ground, but this runs out pretty soon. Notice that the little seed grew leaves very quickly as it needed the leaves to make food so it could grow some more.

You may want to tell them that the plants use water, air and sunlight to make their food and this process is called photosynthesis.

Refer back to the leaves you collected last week. Look at how different the leaves are. Show some leaves that don't look like leaves, e.g. carrot tops, pine needles, grasses, cactus spines.

Make the point that all plants have leaves because all plants need leaves to make their food. But the leaves of different plants can look very different. You may want to spend some time linking the type of leaf to the environment from which it originates.

What next?

If you want to record your findings in a creative way then you could:

- Ages 4–5: match up leaves from the same plant by looking at their shape, size, colour and other features.

- Make your own leaf identification charts. Write notes about how to recognise each leaf, using the proper vocabulary, under each picture.

- Make a treasure hunt for other children in your class. Write clues about the leaves they should look for, taking them from tree to tree around the outside area.

- Write an extra page for the story where a child picks all the leaves off a plant. Describe what happens to the plant. Does it die or grow some more leaves and survive?

- Make a game of leaf bingo by sticking six leaves to a piece of paper. Make sure everyone has a different selection of leaves. One person is the bingo caller. They call out the name of a tree and if you have a leaf from that tree, place a counter on the leaf. The first person to get counters on all their leaves is the winner.

- Write a fact file all about leaves. You could include some information about how to identify leaves, why leaves are important and what happened to our plant when we removed all the leaves.

Look out for evidence of scientific thinking and learning

- The children show curiosity and interest in the leaves and trees.
- The children make observations, e.g. this leaf has three parts.
- The children make links, e.g. the leaves are all green.
- The children ask questions, e.g. is this an oak leaf?
- The children can sort the leaves into groups or species based on their leaf shapes and textures etc.

THINK LIKE A BEE

Story link
The flower was visited by the birds and the insects.

THE SCIENCE: Flowers and plant lifecycles

Many flowering plants are insect pollinated. The flowers must attract the bees or other insects to the plant in order to coat them with pollen. This pollen is carried to the next flower so that the pollen can be transferred. This is called pollination. Pollen grains from one flower will fertilize the eggs in another and once fertilised, the eggs will develop into seeds.

The flowers attract the bees in various ways. Sometimes there is a food reward – nectar – hidden at the base of the flower. Sometimes, the insect will eat some of the pollen but the flower makes plenty so it can spare some as a food reward.

The flowers must signal to the insects that they are ready for pollination. They signal by making nectar and scents to attract the insects. Different insects are attracted to different smells. They also produce brightly coloured petals. The way bees see is a little different to the way we see. They can't really see red – they see it as black. But they can see green, white and blue. They can also see something we can't see – ultra violet (UV). Often petals have stripes, like landing strips, guiding the bee into the flower to the nectar. Sometimes, these stripes only show up under UV light.

Many species of bee are social creatures – they live together in colonies and work together to bring up a large brood of larvae, which are all related to them. Many can communicate the location of a good food source to other bees and they can learn to come back to that source.

Many plants are wind pollinated. Their flowers are less elaborate and less colourful. They won't waste energy producing nectar. Instead, they will invest their energy in making lots and lots of tiny pollen grains, which can be caught by the wind and spread far and wide in the hope that they will reach another flower of the same type. This is why the air is full of pollen on hot summery days.

What do the children need to know?

- Flowers are there to attract animals to visit and carry the pollen to another flower.
- The pollen is needed to make seeds.

ACTIVITIES: Sensing flowers and teaching the bees

You will need:

- flowers with a distinct scent (lavender, roses, sweet peas etc.)
- lemons and oranges
- honey
- other scented objects (e.g. bath bombs or herbs)
- small clean opaque pots
- thin fabric lids and elastic bands
- honey bee feeder (could be home made)
- large pieces of card/cloth – blue green white and red
- access to an outside area
- UV torch (available online for under £10)
- UV glow powder (available online from UV party shops).

Check for allergies to flowers, bees and food before you begin and ask for permission from whoever is in charge of Health and Safety before starting this project.

 # Storify the science

Turn to the page where all the insects and birds are visiting the flower. Ask the children if they know why the birds and the insects have come to visit. Explain that there is pollen in the flower that must be carried to another flower to make a seed. (This will be covered again when the children are older so no need to go into detail with children of this age.)

Also explain that there is often some nectar in the flower to eat and some of the animal visitors will eat the pollen in the flower so they are well paid for their delivery role.

Ask the children if they have noticed any flowers on their way to school. Ask them how they spotted them. Elicit that it is the bright colours that draw the eye. Sometimes, we notice the smell too.

Explain that insects and bees can use the same senses. Pass around a pot with a piece of orange skin inside. Ask the children to tell you what the smell is.

 # Set the challenge – sensing the flowers

You are going to create some scent pots. Your challenge is to make three pots and put a different scent in each. One must be a flower smell.

Put cloth lids on top of your pots and secure them with an elastic band.

Give your three pots to another group and see whether they can find the flower smell.

Can they correctly identify all the scents?

Teacher's top tips

The important skills here are using all the senses to observe. Give the children time to get to know each scent, talk about them and learn to name them.

KEY QUESTIONS to help children to move towards an understanding:

- What would you like to try?
- Why did you choose that one?
- Are they all like that?
- Can you find ones that are the same some way?
- Can you describe this one?
- Which one is easiest to recognise?

Return to the book

Return to the book and look at the tiny seed's enormous fiery red flower. Notice how big the petals are. Explain to the children that bees can see different colours too. One of the colours that they can see really well is blue. Red doesn't show up well for bees – it looks black to them. (Search the internet using the phrase 'What can a bee see?' and you'll find some good images to demonstrate this.)

Explain that bees use the petals to show them where the nectar is. They will often come back to the same plants to feed while the flowers are out. They can learn where the flowers are. Explain that we are going to see whether we can teach the bees where to find some food. Show the children the bee feeder.

 ## Set the challenge – teaching the bees (a whole class activity)

We are going to lay out some colours to see whether the bees can learn which colour has the nectar.

Spread out the differently coloured cloth or card in a sunny patch, out of the wind. Choose a place for each colour and make sure the card or cloth won't blow away.

Place your bee feeder on one of the colours. Keep it there all week, topping it up when the feeder is empty.

After a week, get ready with pens and papers. You can spend some time watching and counting the bees. Do more bees come to the colour where the feeder is?

Without moving the card or cloths, move the feeder to a different colour. Now, start counting how many bees visit each colour. You could do tallies or numbers to show how many bees land on each colour.

Where do the bees land now? Do they keep coming back to the colour where the feeder was last week, even though it has moved?

Did we teach the bees where to find the food?

 ## Teacher's top tips

If you have any children who are really skittish about bees or allergic, this could be set up outside a window so that the children are less likely to come into contact with the bees.

The cloth or card needs to be reasonably large (at least A3) to mimic a cluster of flowers.

The important skills here are observing, recognising and naming the insects that visit the card (bees in particular) and recording the number of bees. You could use counters in a jar or tallies in a table, depending on the ability of your children. You may want to give them a 10 minute slot each or watch and count as a large group.

Bees are less likely to come out in the cold and the rain so let the weather forecast help you choose a good week for this activity.

 ## Finale

You might like to watch a video about bees – there are plenty on the internet. Then explain that bees can see a colour we cannot see.

You could even set a 'bee trail' of UV glow powder around the room (or in a dark den, if you can construct one). Take it in turns to use the UV torch to follow the bee trail. (Adult supervision required to make sure children don't put items marked by the powder in their mouths.)

Return to the book

It is important to note that the book shows a complete life cycle. Now that the flower has been pollinated, it can make seeds of its own that will be blown away on the wind, bringing us back to the beginning of the book.

 ## What next?

If you want to record your findings in a creative way then you could:

- Ages 4–5: make a booklet with coloured pages. Draw the feeder on the page to show which colour you put your feeder on. Write the number of bees that you counted visiting each colour.
- Make a board game with a die with coloured spots on each side. Move on more spaces if you roll the colour that the bees liked best.
- Design a bee feeder that would help feed the bees. Use colours and shapes and scents to make your bee feeder attract lots of bees.

- Write a story about the tiny bee who uses scent and colour to find a good flower to feed from.
- Draw a life cycle for a tiny seed.
- Write another seed story, following the pattern of *The Tiny Seed* story about a different seed.

 ## Look out for evidence of scientific thinking and learning

- The children make decisions about which items to use.
- The children use their senses to identify scents.
- The children make observations, e.g. this smell is stronger.
- The children make links, e.g. my dog can find things by sniffing. The bees are like that with flowers.
- The children ask questions, e.g. can you tell the difference between orange and lemon by smelling?
- The children test ideas to find answers, e.g. can we try teaching the bees to find the food on a different colour card?

———————————

7 *Goldilocks and the Three Bears*
Traditional

Use any picture book version that tells the traditional story

TOPIC PLANNER

Story link	Science: Healthy diet and exercise	Activity	Page
What does Baby look like?	Offspring look like their parents Observing Grouping	Matching families What will you look like when you grow up? Matching families of animals – adult and baby (activity)	126
Looking after a baby?	What do we need to survive? Hygiene Sorting equipment	Visit from a parent and baby Sorting baby equipment into groups (activity)	129
The three bears' healthy lunch	Healthy varied diets Food types Innovate a new story using knowledge of healthy diets	Making healthy sandwiches Using knowledge of food types to innovate a new version of the Goldilocks story (activity)	132–3
The three bears get fit	Exercise	What makes you out of breath? Make up an exercise routine for the bears (investigation)	141–2

WHAT DOES BABY LOOK LIKE?

Story link

Baby bear lives with his mummy and daddy.

THE SCIENCE: Offspring look like their parents

Our natural external appearance is set by our genes. Of course, we can change it with hair dye or glasses but the features we were born with are set by our genes. In every cell in our body we carry a set of these genes. They are templates for our body to make proteins but as everyone's genes are different, the proteins they produce are different and our outward appearances are different as a result.

When animals reproduce sexually, the egg and sperm meet, forming an embryo. So, some of our genes are inherited from our mother and some from our father.

What do the children need to know?

- We look like our parents because we have inherited half of our genes from our mother and half from our father.

ACTIVITY: Matching families

You will need:

- pictures of different bears, e.g. polar bear, panda, black bear and brown bear
- photos of adult and baby animals for matching – there is a lot of this type of resource online. Choose an appropriate number of animals for the level of knowledge of your class. Add a couple that they won't know. You could include: puppy/dog, calf/cow, cygnet/swan, chick/chicken, lamb/sheep, baby/adult human, foal/horse. Less well known ones might be tadpole/frog, caterpillar/butterfly or different types of dog. Really tricky ones might include a new-born kangaroo, hamster, panda or rabbit as these look different when they are still pink and hairless.

Storify the science

Read the whole story of Goldilocks. Then, turn to a page with a picture of all three bears. Ask the children to find ways in which the bears look alike, e.g. their ears or their fur. Ask the children to look for differences, e.g. their sizes.

Show them pictures of other bears – polar bears, pandas and black bears. Ask the children if these bears could be baby bear's parents. Discuss how children look like their parents. Bears have baby bears, pandas have baby pandas and people have baby people. They might be different sizes but the features are similar.

Show the children photos of yourself at different ages. Note how different an adult looks as a teenager, a child and a baby. Show the children photos of your parents and try to spot where your family traits come from.

Ask the children whether they know anything about themselves that is just like their parents. Be aware of any looked-after children who may not be living with parents. It may be necessary to focus on one known family such as your own to make this discussion inclusive for all.

Ask the children to think about what they might look like when they grow up. Will their eye colour change? Will their height change? Will their hair colour change? You could give the children time to draw themselves as adults at this point. Younger children will find it harder to imagine so don't dwell here with little ones.

Find a picture of Goldilocks and show it to the children. Ask them to imagine what her parents might look like. Ask if they think both of her parents will have curly hair. Again, with older children, you could let them draw the parents. Drawing will help them to focus on details such as height and hair and eyes. This often leads to discussion about themselves such as, 'My dad has curly hair but Mummy doesn't. My hair is like Mummy's'. Maybe Goldilocks' dad has curly hair. They might say, 'My dad and I have the same skin tone but my brother is more like my mum'. Encourage healthy discussion.

Now, show them a picture of a different animal, such as a dog. Ask the children what a baby dog is called and what it looks like. Notice that the baby dog has a special name – puppy. Brainstorm other baby names, e.g. bear cub, lamb or kitten.

 # Set the challenge

You are going to match up babies with their parents.

Look carefully at all the pictures of baby animals. Look at their noses and ears and fur and feet. Can you match up the baby animal with the adult animal?

Were there any that you couldn't match up? What made the task so tricky?

 # Teacher's top tips

The important skills here are careful observation and spotting similarities between adult and baby in order to classify or group the animals.

Spend time discussing the way the children match up the adults and babies. Encourage them to look for specific features that are the same in both adult and baby.

You may want to focus on learning the words for the baby animals with older children.

If you want to increase the challenge, include pictures of baby animals that are furless when they are born or are very different as babies, e.g. kangaroos are tiny at birth. You could also throw in a few that don't match up so that the children end up debating where the mystery ones go.

KEY QUESTIONS to help children to move towards an understanding:

- What do you notice?
- Why did you put those together?
- Can you tell me something else that is the same?

 # What next?

If you want to record your findings in a creative way then you could:

- Ages 4–5: show how you matched your animals by putting adults and babies together on a big drawing of a farmyard or zoo. Put each matching pair together in a pen.
- Make a set of cards to use in a game of pairs. Write the animal names and draw or print off pictures of the adult and baby animals, so you can match them with a friend.
- Collect a set of photos that show how you have changed since birth and write your life story so far. You could even include a picture of what you think you'll look like when you grow up and write about the adventures you'll have.

 # Look out for evidence of scientific thinking and learning

- The children look closely at the pictures.
- The children make observations, e.g. you can tell it's a baby rabbit by the ears.
- The children make links, e.g. lots of babies are born without fur.
- The children ask questions, e.g. what do the ears look like?
- The children can sort the pictures into matching adult/baby pairs.

LOOKING AFTER A BABY

Story link

Mummy Bear and Daddy Bear look after Baby Bear.

THE SCIENCE: What do we need to survive?

To stay alive, animals and humans must breathe, stay warm, eat and drink and stay healthy.

We need to **breathe** to get oxygen into our bodies so that we can get the energy from the food we eat and store in our bodies. We can only survive a few minutes without oxygen.

We need to **stay warm** because our bodies are constantly undergoing chemical reactions and these won't work if the temperature is too low or too hot. So, if we get too cold our bodies stop functioning. The length of time we can endure the cold depends on the temperature outside, our clothing and the level of activity. It is possible to get hypothermia in water that is just a few degrees colder than our body temperature.

We need to **eat** to get fuel into our bloodstream and then into the cells where it can be used to produce the energy needed for activity and growth. As our bodies store some energy as fat, we can survive for a few weeks without food.

We need to **drink** so that our cells and organs can function properly. Whatever fluid we drink, it is the water content that is important. Our bodies are about 70 per cent water and we must drink about 1.2 litres of fluid a day to replace the fluids lost by sweating, urinating and even breathing. We can only survive about three days without water.

What do the children need to know?

- Humans need to eat, drink and breathe to stay alive.

ACTIVITY: Visit from a parent and baby

You will need:

- a parent willing to visit the class with their baby
- baby equipment – see chart below for ideas
- photos of lots of baby equipment – enough for one set per group of children. Include baby plates, spoons and toothbrushes and clothes (as adults still need to use the grown up version of items such as these)
- pictures of a bear cub suckling (many on internet)
- picture/video of bear cub riding on mother's back while swimming (some on the internet).

Storify the science

Find a picture of the bear family. Recap (from the last session) that babies look much like their parents. Ask the children what family members do for each other. Discuss the fact that we can give hugs and play games and make each other laugh but there are some really important things parents do for their children that keep them alive. Introduce the idea that all animals, including humans have to do certain things to stay alive – eat, drink and breathe.

Write those three key words on the board.

At this point, ideally, you could introduce your visitor and their baby.

If you are unable to invite a parent and baby into the classroom then you could use a doll and role-play looking after it.

Start by having a good look at the baby. Ask the children what the baby can do. Give the children time to discuss this with a partner. Can they sit up, brush their hair or feed themselves? Discuss how helpless the baby is.

Now show each item of baby equipment and let the children work out why it is needed and how this helps the baby.

Items you might include:

Item	Function
Baby bath	Prevents drowning
Cellular blanket (has gaps in the weave)	Prevents suffocation
Baby bottle	Baby can feed in same way as breastfeeding
Baby clothes	Keeps baby warm
Car seat	Prevents injury
Nappy	Keeps baby clean and germ free
Steriliser	Keeps baby germ free
Play mat	Prevent injury and provides stimulation

 ## Set the challenge

You are going to look at the pictures of baby equipment. You must sort the pictures into three groups:

- equipment to help baby eat, drink, breathe and stay warm;
- equipment to keep baby safe from injury or disease;
- equipment to help baby learn and play.

Did you find any equipment that fits into two groups? Which items do you think are most important? Do you think we need any more groups?

Return to the story.

Look back at the pictures of Baby Bear. Ask the children if he is still a baby like the one that visited the classroom. Baby Bear is eating solid food with a spoon so he is not a young baby – he is a bit older, maybe even at a similar stage to the children in this class.

Ask the children if real baby bears eat porridge when they are born. Show the children pictures of baby bears suckling from their mother (plenty online).

Ask the children if baby bears wear clothes. Discuss how their fur keeps them warm but they are born with very fine hair so they need to huddle together with their mother when they are very young.

Show the children a picture (or video) of bear cubs riding on the back of a mother bear as she swims across a lake. Discuss how the babies might drown if they swam (just like a baby in a bath) so the mother keeps them safe by carrying them.

In this way, show them that all animals must eat, drink, breathe and stay warm to stay alive.

 ## Teacher's top tips

The important skill here is recognising the things we have to do to stay alive.

The children also need to sort the items and recognise how each item helps the baby.

Although the equipment will be largely familiar to the children, they may never have thought about why it is needed so spend time discussing and demonstrating the way it is designed to help the baby.

KEY QUESTIONS to help children to move towards an understanding:

- What do you notice?
- Why is it that shape?
- How could that help the baby?
- What could happen?
- Do you think the baby needs this?
- Which group shall we put it in?

 ## What next?

If you want to record your findings in a creative way then you could:

- Ages 4–5: role-play looking after baby. Show us how you make sure baby is alive, safe and well.

- Write a book called 'Baby Bear Care' for Mummy and Daddy Bear. Explain how to look after a baby bear.

- Role-play being an explorer who is off to find polar bears in the frozen north. Think of all the things you'll need to take with you so you can stay alive and healthy. Pack your rucksack with everything you need. Explain why you chose the items in your rucksack.

- Design a bedroom for baby bears (or baby people). Annotate your design to explain how each part keeps baby safe and well.

Look out for evidence of scientific thinking and learning

- The children show curiosity and interest in the baby and equipment.
- The children use their senses to explore the equipment.
- The children make observations, e.g. the blanket has holes.
- The children make links e.g. all the food equipment is really soft so baby can't hurt itself.
- The children can sort the equipment into groups based on their functions.

THE THREE BEARS' HEALTHY LUNCH

Story link

The bears eat breakfast in the original story. They lunch in the innovated story below but only baby bear eats a varied diet!

THE SCIENCE: Healthy varied diets

There are five main food groups that we need in our diet. While advice from different sources suggests eating differing amounts of each food every day, they all agree that our bodies need a variety of foods to stay healthy as they need a variety of nutrients, vitamins and minerals to function. The food groups are:

- starchy food or carbohydrates, which give us energy. If you chose an unrefined version such as brown bread and rice then there are more nutrients and more fibre left in the foods so they are better for us;

- protein, which gives us the building blocks to form muscles and grow;

- fruit and vegetables, which are packed full of vitamins, minerals and fibre;

- dairy foods such as milk and yoghurt that contain calcium, which is needed to strengthen our teeth and bones;

- fats such as butter and oil, which give us lots of energy and should be eaten in small portions.

Treat foods that are high in fat or sugar or salt, such as cakes, ice cream and crisps don't do our bodies much good so we shouldn't eat them too often. They certainly shouldn't form the basis of our diet. If we eat too much sugar, any left over in our bodies is converted to fat.

These groups in healthy proportions are laid out on the 'Eatwell Plate' which you can find on the internet as a guide to how much of each food group we should consume each day as part of a healthy diet.

N.B. Most foods contain a mixture of food groups, e.g. fruit contains vitamins and minerals but also carbohydrates.

What do the children need to know?

- Different foods give our bodies different nutrients so we should eat a wide range of foods to be healthy.

 # ACTIVITY: Making healthy sandwiches

You will need:

- copies of the 'Eatwell Plate' or another representation of a varied diet. It needs to show pictures of different foods and show how foods are grouped into types

- plenty of adult helpers

- plates and knives

- butter and spread

- brown and white bread

- lettuce, cucumber and tomato slices

- cheese slices

- ham or chicken slices

- jam

- chocolate spread (no nuts)

- tuna

- cress.

N.B. If there are children in your class with allergies, avoid those foods and substitute with something in the same food group. Likewise, alter the selection if there are religious objections to certain foods.

Storify the science

For this session, we need a new story. However, it follows the structure of the original story closely enough to be instantly recognisable to the child. This process of making slight changes to the story models how the children can later change the details to make their own story, as part of their science lesson.

Goldilocks and the Three Bears lunch

Once upon a time, in the middle of a forest, in a beautiful cottage, lived three bears: Daddy Bear, Mummy Bear and Baby Bear.

Daddy Bear was rather wobbly and fat because he only liked to eat sugary foods such as cake and biscuits. Mummy Bear was big and muscly because she only ate protein to build her muscles. But Baby Bear, who ate lots of different foods, was just right.

It had been raining all day and the three bears were just about to have lunch when the rain suddenly stopped and the sun came out.

'Let's go for a walk,' said Mummy Bear, 'before it starts raining again.' So, the three bears left their lunch on the table and went off for walk in the forest.

Just then, Goldilocks arrived at the three bears' cottage. She was dripping wet as she had been caught in the rain and she was very, very hungry. She knew she ought not go into the house. Last time she went into the three bears' cottage, she had eaten their breakfast and they were very cross. But she was getting cold and her tummy was rumbling. So, she decided to go in and see what smelled so good. Naughty little Goldilocks!

There, on the table were three plates. On Daddy's plate there were a lot of sugary foods, which made Daddy Bear rather wobbly and fat. There was a large slice of cake and a biscuit.

On Mummy's plate, there was lots of protein to make her muscles big and strong. There was a boiled egg, a chicken leg and some ham.

On Baby Bear's plate, there were lots of different foods, which kept Baby Bear healthy. There was a jacket potato (hot and steaming), a pile of tasty cheese and a large spoonful of peas and sweetcorn. It smelled so good. She couldn't help herself and, before she knew it, she had eaten it all up.

Just then, the door flew open. There stood the three bears, dripping wet, just like Goldilocks, and Mummy and Daddy Bear were puffing and panting.

'If you could run faster, we wouldn't have got so wet!' said Baby Bear.

'Perhaps you should eat a better diet like Baby Bear!' said Goldilocks as she scampered out the back door.

'Has she been eating my lunch?' panted Daddy Bear, a little out of breath.

'Has she been eating my lunch? ' panted Mummy Bear, angrily.

'No,' cried Baby Bear. 'But she's been eating my lovely lunch and she's eaten it all up!'

The next day, the three bears went to the market to buy lots of different healthy foods so they could all eat as well as Baby Bear. And when they got home, they went off to woods to exercise. So if Goldilocks came back, they'd be able to catch her before she ate their dinner.

Start by telling (or reading) this story to the children. Then create a map of the story – see facing page.

Help the children learn to tell the story themselves. I use a technique called 'Hear Map Step Speak' based on the work of Storytelling Schools. You can find more about these techniques on the Storytelling Schools website.

Once the children are familiar with the story and can tell it with you, with actions, they are ready to move on.

Give out copies of the 'Eatwell Plate' or something similar and look at the foods represented on it.

Practise finding foods in the different categories. Ask the children to find the foods on Mummy Bear's plate. Notice that they are all proteins that make us big and strong but we need other foods too.

Ask the children to find the foods on Daddy Bear's plate. Notice that these are not even on the 'Eatwell Plate'. They are in a section of treat foods that you shouldn't eat very often. No wonder Daddy Bear is rather wobbly and fat. Ask the children whether they think Daddy Bear's food will make him muscly and strong. Ask them if they think Daddy Bear's food will keep him healthy.

Discuss what they know about drinking milk to keep teeth and bones strong and eating vegetables and fruit to stay healthy.

Ask the children to find Baby Bear's food. Notice that he has carbohydrate for energy, protein for his muscles and vegetables to keep him healthy. Note that cheese is also dairy. Also note that a glass of milk would make the lunch even more varied.

Keep looking at the different food categories until you feel the children are familiar with the names of the groups and understand that they need foods from every group and they shouldn't have treat foods very often.

Set the challenge

Wash your hands!

You are going to use your knowledge of food groups to create a healthy sandwich that has foods from as many groups as possible. If you like, you can eat your sandwich at the end to see how good healthy food can taste.

When you make your sandwich, think about:

* which foods will be good for your body;
* how much of each food you should use;
* how many different foods you can include at once;
* how those foods will taste when you put them together!

Try your sandwich. What did it taste like? How healthy do you think it was? What else could you have with your sandwich to make it a really varied lunch?

Teacher's top tips

The important skills here are recognising the food types and being able to sort food into those groups. The children must also solve a problem using this knowledge as they have to create a varied and healthy lunch using the foods.

If you do this activity with the whole class do have a few extra adults primed with the key questions as the main purpose of the activity is to generate discussion about food groups. Left to their own devices, you'll have 30 jam sandwiches with a cucumber slice on the side. It's just too tempting!

KEY QUESTIONS to help children to move towards an understanding:

* What do you want to try?
* Why did you choose that?
* Which food groups have you already got?
* What else would you like to add?
* Which ones do you think are healthy?
* How will this food help our bodies?
* What do you like to eat?

Return to the story

Look back at the story map. Use sticky notes to cover the parts of the map where the meals are mentioned. You could also cover Goldilocks.

Demonstrate how to use the 'Eatwell Plate' to choose different foods for the bears. Choose a different protein for Mummy Bear's plate and draw it on the sticky note. Choose a different treat

food for Daddy Bear and a varied meal of carbohydrate, protein and vegetables for Baby Bear and put them on the sticky notes too.

Now, imagine a different character who has a name based on a physical characteristic. It could be a boy, e.g. Freddy Fastfoot and draw him with speedy trainers on his feet on the sticky note covering Goldilocks on the map.

Now, re-tell the story with these innovated details.

— *Once upon a time . . .*

— *. . . Just then, Freddy Fastfoot arrived at the three bears' cottage. He was dripping wet as he had been caught in the rain and he was very, very hungry . . .*

— *. . . There, on the table were three plates. On Daddy's plate there was lots of sugary foods, which made Daddy Bear rather wobbly and fat. There was a piece of cheese cake and a muffin.*

— *On Mummy's plate, there was lots of protein to make her muscles big and strong. There was a lamb chop, a chicken wing and some beans.*

— *On Baby Bear's plate, there were lots of different foods, which kept Baby Bear healthy and strong. There was some pasta (hot and steaming), some tuna and a large spoonful of carrots and broccoli. It smelled so good. He couldn't help himself and before he knew it he had eaten it all up . . .*

Give the children a pre-drawn story map on a worksheet. Fill in most of the story but leave empty circles where you put the sticky notes. Let the children fill in their own ideas for the character name and the three meals. Encourage them to use the 'Eatwell Plate' to help them choose the right foods. With younger children, work in groups and let the adult helper draw one map for the whole group.

 # What next?

If you want to record your findings in a creative way then you could:

- Ages 4–6: role-play being Bears. You could go the market and buy healthy foods so you can catch anyone who tried to steal your dinner. You could even write a healthy shopping list.

- Have a healthy class picnic!

- Write the story you innovated on your story map. Make sure you practise telling it first so you know what to write!

- Role-play your story and make a video of it.

- Create a Three Bears' Lunch Game where you have to be the first to collect foods from every food group. When you've got them all you can chase Goldilocks!

Look out for evidence of scientific thinking and learning

- The children use their senses to explore the foods.
- The children choose their own ingredients to make a healthy sandwich.
- The children make observations, e.g. there are seeds in the brown bread.
- The children ask questions, e.g. why is jam in the treat section as there is fruit in it?
- The children sort the foods into groups.
- The children can review their own sandwich and decide whether it makes a healthy meal or not.

THE THREE BEARS GET FIT

Story link

The three bears have to exercise so they can chase Goldilocks next time she tries to steal their dinner.

THE SCIENCE: Exercise

Any exercise that makes us out of breath will be making our heart pump. Our heart is a muscle and it is exercised and grows stronger when we do anything that increases our heart rate. This is called cardiovascular exercise.

As we exercise, our muscles are using more oxygen as we use up the food in our bodies to release the energy. To get more oxygen into our bodies we have to breathe more rapidly and more deeply – we puff and pant.

Other exercises may work specific parts of the body, strengthening the muscles but we need to do cardiovascular exercise in order to be fit.

What do the children need to know?

- Regular exercise makes our heart and body strong and keeps us fit and healthy.
- Adults should exercise regularly.
- Children need to be active and play outside.

INVESTIGATION: What makes you out of breath?

You will need:

- space to run around and set up obstacle courses
- safe hurdles
- safe climbing wall or climbing frame
- cones/markers
- balls
- skipping ropes
- balance beams
- hoops
- clipboard
- record sheet

RECORD SHEET		
Exercise	Does it make you out of breath?	Does any part of you feel tired?
Bouncing a ball	✗	✗

 Storify the science

Retell the story from last week – the innovated version or the original. When you get to the last part about the bears going off into the woods to exercise, ask the children what kind of exercises might make the bears fitter. Discuss exercises that real bears could do as well as human exercises, such as running. Ask the children how we can tell whether an exercise is working our body hard. Elicit that we puff and pant when our bodies are working hard, our heart pumps harder and we go red.

Get the children dressed in appropriate clothing and go outside and look at all the equipment. Talk about the kinds of exercises you can do with it.

Allow the children some time to explore the equipment and come up with exercises they can do with it. Ask them which made them out of breath.

Show them the record sheet and show them how to fill in the exercise they are doing, e.g. bouncing a ball. Then ask a child to bounce a ball for a minute. Ask if the child is out of breath and if any part of them feels tired. Mark their observations on the sheet. (With younger children you may just want to explore the exercises and then talk about them afterwards.)

Set the challenge

You are going to try lots of different exercises to see how they might help make the three bears fit enough to catch that naughty Goldilocks. When you try an exercise, think about:

- which part of the body the bears need to exercise in order to catch Goldilocks;
- how tired the exercise makes you feel;
- how hard it makes you breathe;
- how each part of your body feels afterwards;
- which exercises would help you get fit.

Don't forget to have a little rest between each exercise!

Which exercises do you think the bears should do if they want to be fit enough to catch Goldilocks? How often should they do these exercises? Write an exercise routine for the bears.

Teacher's top tips

The important skills here are observing the effect of exercise on our bodies and choosing the ones that make us out of breath and the ones that exercise our legs, as we need these for running.

They may decide that the bears need to exercise their arms so they can catch Goldilocks and hang on to her. Celebrate that kind of thinking!

If you have heart monitors and you feel your children can understand what they are measuring, then you could measure heart rate for different exercises.

KEY QUESTIONS to help children to move towards an understanding:

- What do you want to try?
- Why did you choose that?
- Can you find something that gets you out of breath?
- Do they all make you just as tired?
- What else shall we try?
- What do you notice about your breathing/body?
- Do all the exercises do that?

What next?

If you want to record your findings in a creative way then you could:

- Ages 4–5: role-play being Baby Bear showing his parents how to do the exercise routine you designed.
- Write a mini book for bears on suitable exercises for staying fit.

- Write another story where Goldilocks comes back and finds the bears have left their evening meal on the table. All the meals are healthy and varied. Goldilocks starts to eat Baby Bear's meal but the bears come home and this time they are fit and healthy and can catch her because they have been exercising. Goldilocks ends up as dinner!

- Make a snakes and ladders style board game. Healthy choices such as healthy food and exercise take you up the ladders but eating cake and lazing about takes you down the snake again.

 ## Look out for evidence of scientific thinking and learning

- The children engage in the activity, exploring the equipment.
- The children think of ideas to try out.
- The children make observations, e.g. skipping makes me really out of breath.
- The children make links, e.g. all the jumping exercises make me out of breath.
- The children ask questions, e.g. does skipping make everyone out of breath?
- The children test ideas to find answers, e.g. I think skipping and running along at the same time will make me really out of breath.
- The children can sort the exercises into those that make them out of breath and those that don't.

———————————————

8 *The Odd Egg*

Emily Gravett (2008)

TOPIC PLANNER

Story link	Science: Animal life cycles	Activity	Page
Laying eggs	Why do birds make nests? Knowing if eggs are alive	Making safe places for eggs Comparing materials to find the best ones to keep the egg safe (activity)	147
Incubating	Birds need warmth to stay alive Solving a problem	Finding ways to keep warm (investigation)	151–2
Hatching all kinds of eggs	There are egg layers of all kinds	Observing eggs and hatching Observing chick, caterpillars and tadpoles emerging from eggs (activity) Researching other animals that lay eggs	157–8
Looking after our local birds	Different birds eat different foods Identifying and naming local birds	Making bird feeders to attract local birds Identifying and naming local birds and describing how they get their food (activity)	162

N.B. If you have children with egg or nut allergies in the class you may not be able to do some of the sessions.

LAYING EGGS

Story link

All the birds lay an egg, except Duck.

THE SCIENCE: Why do birds make nests?

The simple answer is that birds create a cup-shaped nest or dip in the ground to stop their eggs rolling away so that they can sit on the entire clutch of eggs and keep them at the right temperature for the chicks inside to develop.

The nest must be a rounded shape to cradle the eggs without puncturing them. Many birds ensure the inside of their nest is very smooth and soft. Some will line their nests with feathers to provide insulation to keep the eggs from losing valuable heat.

Eggs are almost spherical in shape. Spheres are stronger shapes than cubes and more comfortable to lay than shapes with corners and flat sides. All animal eggs are rounded in this way. Many bird eggs are mostly oval and tapered at one end. This shape is easier to squeeze out (blunt end first) and it has an added advantage: an egg will tend to roll around in a circle rather than roll away, so this shape is common in birds who nest on cliff edges.

What do the children need to know?

*   Nests provide a place to hold all the eggs in a clutch where they won't roll away so the mother bird can sit on them to keep them warm.
*   They are often lined with soft materials to protect the eggs and prevent breakages.

ACTIVITY: Making safe places for eggs

You will need:

*   raw eggs (or boiled and in plastic bag if there are allergies in class) – one per child plus a few extras
*   bright light/torch
*   a plate
*   a tray
*   cloths to wipe up the mess!
*   an egg box
*   soft materials

*   hard materials
*   sticks
*   stones
*   feathers
*   moss
*   grasses
*   Lego bricks
*   small boxes, e.g. shoe boxes
*   sellotape

Storify the science

Check for children with egg allergies and make sure they are made safe for this lesson.

Read the book *The Odd Egg* to the children. Return to the first page where the robin and the flamingo have made nests for their eggs. The pictures of both nests are roughly accurate and as the robin and the flamingo are the most distinctive nest builders of this group of birds, you need only look at these. Ask the children why birds build a nest. Give them time to talk to a partner and listen to all their ideas.

Show the children a raw egg from an egg box of ordinary shop-bought eggs. Ask them what might be inside. Listen to all their answers, real and imaginary, appreciating them all. Ask the children whether they think this egg is alive. Discuss how some eggs develop into chicks (or other animals) and yet others we eat and they are not alive. Ask them how you might find out. Elicit that opening the egg might kill it.

Show them how chicken farmers will put a bright light up to the egg to see if they can see dark patches inside. Your egg won't have any. Crack the egg and look at the contents with the children. Point out that the yolk is a really good source of food for lots of animals, including us, because it is there to nourish the developing chick.

Discuss how they only contain a live chick if they come from a chicken farm where there is a male chicken (cockerel/rooster) to fertilise the eggs. Only fertile eggs develop into chicks.

Ask your adult helper to bring you another egg. Tell them you need one that isn't broken for your science lesson. They should bring the egg to you on a flat plate where the egg can roll around. Call out instructions to the adult helper to be careful but prime the adult to let the egg drop to the floor and break (preferably on a well-positioned tray rather than the carpet).

Look shocked. Ask the children why it broke. Discuss that a really hard egg would trap the chick inside so they have be breakable. So, the mother egg must take care of them by laying them in a safe place. Discuss how nests are safe. You may need to show them pictures if the children have little experience of birds nesting. Note how the nests are rounded to keep the eggs inside and often lined with soft materials to protect the eggs and keep them warm when the mother bird is sitting on them.

Show the children some more raw shop-bought eggs. Give them spots like the story if you like. Notice how they roll around on a flat surface.

Give each child/pair/group a small box.

 # Set the challenge

You are going to make a nest for your egg to keep it safe.

Choose things to add things to your box so that the egg won't roll around in the box or break, if the box is dropped.

Before you start building a nest, look carefully at all the materials. Feel them and see which ones will be good for making some kind of nest structure and which will be good for lining to make it soft.

Does your nest hold the egg well? Will it protect the egg if the nest is bumped or blown in the wind?

 ## Teacher's top tips

The important skills here are building some kind of egg box structure to go within the box to keep the egg still and then choosing materials to line the box to provide the padding.

You may want to put boiled eggs or fake rubber eggs out so that the children can test their nests as they build them.

If you want to make it more of a competition for older children, you could put a raw egg in a small sealed bag into their box and drop the box from a set height, to see if it survives a fall. The bag will prevent the materials from getting messy in case of disaster.

KEY QUESTIONS to help children to move towards an understanding:

- What do you want to try?
- Why did you choose that?
- Can you describe this material?
- Where will you put it?
- How will you keep the egg safe?

- Which is the better one to use?
- Why do you think that?
- What about this one?
- What else would you like to use?

 ## Finale

Look online for some footage of birds using nest boxes. You'll see that even birds that choose holes and hollows to nest in rather than building nests will collect lining materials to protect the eggs.

 ## What next?

If you want to record your findings in a creative way then you could:

- Ages 4–5: stick a piece of each material you used onto a sheet of card and write a word to describe why you chose it, e.g. soft.
- Create a worksheet with pictures of each bird and the nest they build, keeping sizes to scale. Match up birds to the nests they build.
- Write instructions for Duck on how to make a nest for his egg.
- Take a photo or make a detailed drawing of the nest you made and label all the things you used and why you chose them.
- Role-play being the robin and explain to Duck why he should build a nest for his egg.

Look out for evidence of scientific thinking and learning

- The children find a way to protect the egg.

- The children make observations, e.g. this material is spongy so it will protect the eggs.

- The children make links, e.g. I can't put any of these hard bricks with corners next to the egg as they might crack it.

- The children ask questions, e.g. are feathers softer than wool?

- The children test ideas to find answers, e.g. I think I need to make an egg holder inside my box to keep it still so I'm going to try using this material.

- The children can sort the materials into those that are good at protecting the egg and those that are not.

- The children review how well their design worked.

INCUBATING

Story link
The birds all sit on their eggs.

THE SCIENCE: Birds need warmth to stay alive

Birds are warm blooded so they need to have warm bodies in order to stay alive. In the same way, their offspring need to be kept in a warm environment in order to survive and develop. Other egg layers, such as fish, have cold blood and get their body heat from the environment. Their eggs can develop at lower temperatures. Some reptiles lay eggs in a specific location, with a stable temperature, as this is necessary for development while others can tolerate large fluctuations in temperature.

Oddly, as 'cold-blooded' animals will get their heat from the environment, in a hot environment, their blood can actually be warmer than the blood of a 'warm-blooded' animal that is generating its own body heat.

Most birds sit on their clutch of eggs in order to use their own body heat to incubate them. The body temperature of the bird is therefore the right temperature for incubating the eggs, in most species. Usually, the female will incubate the eggs but, in some birds, the males play a part too, taking a turn at sitting on the eggs or playing a more significant role.

If eggs are incubated outside a nest, they will need a constant heat source. This can be provided by an incubator and then you can watch the eggs hatch in the classroom, which is a magical experience. In addition to heat, the incubator keeps the eggs moist, which makes the shells easier to break open during hatching.

What do the children need to know?

- Birds' eggs must be kept warm in order to hatch.

 ## INVESTIGATION: Finding ways to keep warm

You will need:

- enough recently boiled eggs for one per pair (still warm but not too hot to touch). Check for egg allergies in the class
- gently heated wheat bags or baked potatoes (if you can't use eggs)
- materials of different types, including some that are good thermal insulators and will keep the egg warm, e.g. fleece and some poor thermal insulators such as netting that will let all the heat escape.
- access to warm and cold places such as a sunny windowsill and a dark corner
- egg boxes
- metal skewer (adult use only)
- thermometer or temperature probe and data logger
- a hatching programme that supplies fertilised eggs that are due to hatch, an incubator and a brood box where the chicks can be housed in the classroom for a week or so. I have used www.livingeggs.co.uk and found them to be very helpful and reliable. This company operates across the UK and supplies ten eggs, most of which will hatch within a couple of days of arriving. You do have to pay for the programme but it is worth every penny. Other hatching programmes are available!

N.B. The chicks do go back to the farm at the end of the two weeks. Some will be food. Others will produce eggs. I am always honest with my children about this as I think meat eaters should know how their food is produced and care about the welfare of the animals. I tell them we are farmers for two weeks. However, you know your class and you may want to handle things differently.

 ## Storify the science

Look at the page where Duck is sitting on the egg. Ask the children why they think he is sitting on it. Find out what they know about birds incubating their eggs.

Show them some footage of birds sitting on their eggs. You may be lucky enough to find a live feed from a nesting box that you could leave running in the classroom for children to watch.

The type of bird is not important. Just watch how the adult bird keeps track of her eggs and makes sure they are tucked under her body.

Ask the children to imagine what it would feel like to be sat on by their parents. Point out that birds are quite lightweight as their bones are often hollow so they can fly. You might feel squished but it would be warm!

Ask the children whether they think crocodiles sit on their eggs. You may want to stop here to find out whether they sit on their eggs or show a video of crocodiles burying their eggs and leaving them.

Ask the children why birds sit on their eggs if the crocodile doesn't. Introduce the idea that the birds don't always live in hot climates. They can survive in cold places because their body can create its own heat and they have feathers to keep that heat inside. Crocodiles haven't got fur or feathers. They are cold blooded and need the sun to keep them warm so the sun can keep the eggs warm too.

Look at Duck. Ask whether he could keep that enormous egg warm by sitting on it and using just his body heat.

Ask what else he could use to keep the egg warm? A woolly jumper? A hot water bottle? A radiator?

 # Set the challenge

Duck has a problem. All the other birds are big enough to sit on their eggs and cover them with their body and feathers. Duck's egg is too big for him. He needs you to help him to find a way to keep his egg warm.

You might want to make something to keep the egg warm or you might think of somewhere to put the egg. You'll need to be able to leave the egg there for an hour.

Your teacher will help you to use a thermometer or temperature probe to find out how warm your egg is, once an hour has gone by.

If you find a good way to keep the egg warm, you can tell Duck all about it.

You teacher will put one warm egg on her desk so we can see how cold the egg might get in an hour, without our help.

 # Teacher's top tips

The important skill here is finding a solution to the problem. Birds will use their own body heat and insulating materials to line the nest so that the heat isn't lost. The children may choose to wrap the egg up and then put it somewhere warm too. It doesn't matter how the problem is solved as long as the egg is kept warm.

The egg boxes may prove useful as a way to stop the egg rolling away.

The best time to tackle this problem would be in the session before lunch so that the eggs can be left undisturbed for an hour before you come back to check on them.

You may need a metal skewer to break a small hole in the shell to insert a thermometer or temperature probe to check the temperature.

Wherever possible, let the children have a go at reading the temperature. If you have a data logger with a temperature probe connected to a projector – you can share the results with the class as you check them.

Boiled eggs straight from the pan will be too hot. Boil them well, before the lesson, then wrap them up and place in an insulated bag to keep them warm until you are ready to use them.

Remember to check children's allergies before using raw or cooked eggs in the classroom where the children may come into contact with them.

Some classes like competition – if so, give prizes for the warmest egg after an hour. If they will be put off by having one winner, then any egg that is warmer than the one left on the teacher's desk, uncovered, has solved the problem.

Some children will cover their eggs in a thermal insulator such as fleece and also place the wrapped egg in a warm place such as on a radiator. The fleece will trap the warm air inside but also block the warmth from the radiator from getting into the egg (as the insulator slows the transfer of heat from one side to the other). You may want to discuss this with the children and work out whether they needed to do both by trying an unwrapped egg near the radiator.

Do check whether it is safe to put items on the radiators in your classroom. Some heating systems have to be kept clear for safety reasons.

Just because they have found one solution to the problem doesn't mean their minds will stop ticking and they may want to try out further ideas at a later date. If you can accommodate their curiosity, then do let them keep exploring and try out their ideas over the following days.

KEY QUESTIONS to help children to move towards an understanding:

- What do you want to try?
- Why did you choose that?
- Can you describe this material?
- Where will you put it?
- How will you keep the egg safe?
- Which is the better one to use?
- Why do you think that?
- What about this one?

 Finale

Once you have checked all the eggs to see whether they are warm and discussed the ideas that work, return to the book.

Ask the children if they would like to hatch some eggs and show them the incubator. In my school, this causes excitement and delight that can be heard down the corridors!

Using the information supplied with the programme, explain how the incubator will keep the eggs at exactly the right temperature. For chick eggs, this is around 37°C. The incubator is also kept moist by trays of water at the base so that the eggshells are easier to break open. You may have to turn the eggs like a mother hen or you may be told to leave the eggs lying still. Then prepare to spend the next few days with children in a state of high excitement and engagement as the eggs begin to hatch. If you are lucky enough to have one hatch during school hours, drop everything and watch. It can be over very quickly and is something the children remember forever.

 # What next?

If you want to record your findings in a creative way then you could:

- Ages 4–5: create a display of your egg incubating ideas and write labels to explain what you chose to do.
- Write instructions for Duck explaining how to keep his egg warm, using the successful ideas tested by your class.
- Write a letter to Duck to tell him what you found out.
- Pretend to be an Egg Expert. Give a short talk on the method you used to keep the egg warm and how the incubator works.
- Film the eggs in the incubator and, later, film them hatching. Write a script that could be read out as the voiceover for the films you have made. Use an app such as iMovie to create a nature documentary about your eggs hatching.

 # Look out for evidence of scientific thinking and learning

- The children think of their own ideas.
- The children make observations, e.g. the carpet is warm where the sun is shining on it.
- The children make links, e.g. my winter jumpers are all thick. Maybe a thick jumper keeps you warmer.
- The children ask questions, e.g. will it get warmer if I rub it?
- The children test ideas to find answers, e.g. I'm going to try putting mine near the radiator.
- The children can sort the materials into those that are good at keeping the egg warm and those that are not.
- The children review how effective their idea was at keeping the egg warm.

HATCHING ALL KINDS OF EGGS

Story link

All the eggs hatch.

THE SCIENCE: There are egg layers of all kinds

Some animals lay eggs (oviparous), while others give birth to live young (viviparous). In an egg, the developing animal usually has some kind of yolk to sustain it until hatching. In animals that bear live young, the developing animal is nourished by the mother's body.

The type of egg laid can vary from very simple small eggs that have no shell, and the yolk is spread throughout the egg, to large shelled eggs with a yolk sac.

Caterpillar eggs have a distinct shape, which is different for each species. All have a waxy shell with a hole at the top, through which the sperm can pass to fertilise the egg and this also allows water and air into the developing egg. When adult butterflies mate, the female stores the sperm inside her body until she is ready to lay her eggs. The eggs are usually laid on a plant that the caterpillar can eat and then left alone to develop and hatch (many will be eaten by predators). There is a yolk inside the egg and often the hatching caterpillar eats its own eggshell too.

Frogspawn is made of many eggs lumped together. There is no shell as the eggs are laid in water. Oxygen and water can reach the tadpole through the jelly outer layer.

What do the children need to know?

- Eggs may contain a living and developing animal, if they have been fertilised.
- The egg protects the developing animal and contains food to sustain it until it hatches.
- Some eggs have shells, others do not.

ACTIVITY: Observing eggs and hatching

You will need:

- large papier mâché egg made by covering a large balloon with newspaper strips soaked in flour and water paste. This can take a few days to dry so make it well in advance. Paint it to look like the egg in the book
- eggs made from bicarbonate of soda, containing hidden plastic animals (instructions below)
- pipettes
- bowls or paint trays
- pots of vinegar and water
- caterpillar eggs, food and small net butterfly enclosure – these can be ordered from companies such as Insect Lore, as an inexpensive package
- frogspawn from your school pond
- a tank of pond water and a few large rocks, located in a cool, shady area of the room or playground; the tadpoles need to be kept cool. They will eventually develop lungs, so they'll need to be able to sit out of the water, on the rocks, to breathe air
- hand lenses
- hand held magnifier.

 ## Storify the science

Before the children arrive, create a kind of nest in the classroom out of unusual items, e.g. shredded coloured paper and glitter. Place it somewhere very visible but not easily knocked. Ignore it and let the children tell you about it when they come in. Act surprised and then call them all to the carpet to find out more. Prime your other adults to be equally surprised and ask one of them to tell you they forgot to shut the door/window last night. Decide, with the class that an animal must have come into the classroom and laid it overnight and that the class should look after it until it hatches.

Discuss what might be inside.

Using what you know from last week's problem solving, come up with a way to keep the egg warm and leave it in a sensible place in the classroom to hatch.

Be playful. Check on the egg regularly and listen for sounds of movement inside.

Ask the children what they know about other creatures that lay eggs. Explore the idea that other animals come from eggs too and not all eggs have hard shells.

If you are able, show them frogspawn and caterpillar eggs. Discuss with the children whether these eggs are like the chick eggs. Use a hand held magnifier to project close-up images of the spawn and the eggs onto your screen. Discuss what might come out of these eggs.

Avoid telling the children what will come out of the eggs. Act as if you don't know and you are interested to see what happens.

If they suggest wildly unlikely ideas, treat those ideas with great respect and then look for evidence as to whether that is possible. But avoid discounting their ideas altogether.

Set the challenge

You are going to observe all the eggs in the classroom carefully, as they hatch.

Make sure you observe the eggs before they hatch and after they have hatched. You may be lucky enough to see one actually hatching.

Observing is different from looking. When we look, we might not notice everything. To observe you'll need to look closely and for a long time, until you are sure you have noticed everything. You also need to use your brain to think about what you are observing and to ask questions about it.

You may need a magnifying glass or magnifier to observe everything.

You may want to write down what you notice or draw it so that you can remember all the details.

Look for:

- patterns
- colours
- shapes

- textures
- movement inside the egg
- what comes out of the egg.

 # Teacher's top tips

The important skill here is observation so allow time to properly look and then allow more time later to look again to see whether there are changes.

Guide the children through the process of looking closely with a magnifying glass to see the fine details and encourage them to discuss what they see so that they can look for details that other children mention.

Provide books and other research materials, posters and access to websites about animals that lay eggs so that they can find out more about eggs and maybe identify the odd egg in the classroom.

Notice that an animal comes out of a fertilised egg and this will develop into an adult that lays eggs in the same way. The animal that hatches out may look like a miniature version of the adult or it may have a different form. Make sure that you spend time, at the end of the week, discussing the life cycles of the animals you are observing

KEY QUESTIONS to help children to move towards an understanding:

- What did you see?
- Do they all look like that?
- What can you see through the magnifying glass?
- Can you describe it?
- What is different about this one?

Little extras

A week in advance, prepare some bicarbonate of soda eggs. (This ingredient is much cheaper if bought at your local 'cash and carry' wholesaler.)

1 kg of bicarbonate of soda will make 30 eggs.

First, mix up the bicarbonate of soda with just enough water to make a paste. Next, take a small plastic animal and mould the paste around the animal into an egg shaped ball, hiding the animal inside. Wear gloves for this, as it is an alkali and can harm your skin.

Leave the eggs to harden. It will take a week for them to thoroughly dry out.

Now, they are ready to be 'hatched' by the children. Place each egg in a bowl or paint tray and ask the children to try to 'hatch' the eggs. Demonstrate by dripping some water, using a pipette, onto the eggs. Have pots of water and vinegar available. The water will soak in, while the vinegar will react with the bicarbonate of soda, producing bubbles of carbon dioxide.

If you put different animals inside each egg, the children will be motivated to find what hatches out of theirs. If you can, try to avoid putting mammals inside the eggs as they are born as live young. Instead, choose dinosaurs and other reptiles, insects and birds.

The children may break up the eggs physically, which speeds up the dissolving process too. They may ask to try other liquids in the classroom such as milk or paint. As long as the liquid is safe for use with the children, let them try out their ideas.

Thanks to Sarah Bearchell (*Sarah's Adventures in Science*) for this activity.

 ## Finale

At the end of the week of observations, make cracks in the papier maché egg and choose a time when the children are out of the classroom to have the egg hatch. Crack it right open. If you want it to be more believable, paint inside it to hide the newsprint and leave to dry overnight.

You could leave it empty or place a suitably large and unfamiliar stuffed animal of your choice in the egg for the children to find.

Let the children find the hatched egg and bring it to the carpet to discuss. It had a hard shell – what do you know about animals with hard shells?

You could then use this as inspiration for developing a story about the odd egg that was laid in their classroom, the animal that hatched out and the havoc it caused in school. You could ask members of staff to run into your class and describe the animal they've just seen in school, causing havoc. Have fun with it.

What next?

If you want to record your findings in a creative way then you could:

- Ages 4–5: learn a poem or song about what you saw, e.g.

  > Ten little eggs all cosy and warm
  >
  > Ten little chicks are beginning to form
  >
  > One little chick goes tap tap tap
  >
  > One little egg goes crack crack crack
  >
  > Nine little chicks . . .

- Complete a mini book labelled with one day of the week on each page, writing down what the egg looks like each day.

- Create a scientific log book, noting what each egg/animal looks like on each day that you observe.

- Make your own papier mâché eggs and paint them with a distinctive pattern. then write a story about what came out of your odd egg.

- Draw and label a life cycle for all the eggs you observed.

Look out for evidence of scientific thinking and learning

- The children try their own ideas to 'hatch' the bicarbonate of soda eggs.

- The children make observations, e.g. this egg has lines on it.

- The children make links, e.g. the smaller animals come out of smaller eggs.

- The children ask questions, e.g. will the bicarbonate of soda egg 'hatch' more quickly if I pour the whole pot of vinegar on it?

- The children test ideas to find answers, e.g. I'm going to try dripping milk on the bicarbonate of soda egg to see if that makes it 'hatch' faster.

- The children can review which method made the bicarbonate of soda eggs 'hatch' faster.

LOOKING AFTER OUR LOCAL BIRDS

Story link
Duck knits a scarf.

THE SCIENCE: Different birds eat different foods

The shape of the beak of the bird will give you some clues about what it eats. Birds have adapted to make use of all kinds of food sources from flower nectar to ants. As their beak is their primary tool for accessing their food, their beaks are shaped according to the food they eat.

To find out about the birds in your local area, you could use the RSPB website which has a wealth of information about what a bird looks like, where it can be found and what it eats.

What do the children need to know?

• Children should be able to recognise and name birds that inhabit their local environment.

ACTIVITY: Making bird feeders

You will need:

• yoghurt pots

• lard

• string

• access to the RSPB website or other research materials that can be used to identify birds and provide information on what they eat

• bird food appropriate for the birds in your local area.

N.B. You may not be able to use nuts in the classroom if children have allergies.

Storify the science

Look back at the book and dwell on the page where Duck is knitting. Ask the children why Duck might be knitting. Look at the owl – he has been teaching his baby to recognise dogs. Discuss how parents look after their offspring. Ask the children why they do that. Elicit that it helps their offspring to survive.

Look again at the picture. Can they name all of the birds in the picture? Ask them which of the birds they ever see in real life and which they might see in the school grounds.

Go outside and spend some time looking and listening. Find evidence of birds – feathers, sightings, birdsong, droppings (encourage looking but not touching). Ask the children to name any birds they can see. Then use a website (e.g. RSPB) to find out more about those birds and identify any birds that were seen but could not be named.

You might like to invite a keen bird spotter into the classroom for this session so you can get help with identification of birds and their songs.

Once you have ascertained which birds are local to your school, find out what they eat. This could be an independent research task for older children or an adult led group activity for younger ones.

 # Set the challenge

You are going to attract some birds into your school garden/outside area by providing the food they like to eat.

First, decide which bird you would like to attract.

Next, find out which food they eat.

Then, collect up the right foods and make them into a seed cake – your adult will show you how.

Once your seed cake is made, choose a suitable place to hang it up, where you can see the birds that visit and prepare to observe the birds. It may take a week for the birds to find the food so try to be patient.

 # Teacher's top tips

The important skill here is recognising and naming the birds in your local area so make sure you find out in advance which birds are common so you can stock up on the right bird food.

There are lots of seed cake recipes on the internet. Most involve softening lard and pressing the seeds into it and then hardening the cake in a mould, such as a yoghurt pot, in the fridge. If the yoghurt pot has a string threaded through it, then you can tie the cake to a tree. Do follow recipes carefully to avoid harming the birds.

You'll probably want lots of adult help with making the seed cakes so work in small groups.

KEY QUESTIONS to help children to move towards an understanding:

- What do you want to try?
- Why did you choose that?
- Where will you put it?

- Why do you think that?
- What about this one?
- What else would you like to use?

What next?

If you want to record your findings in a creative way then you could:

- Ages 4–5: prepare a bird spotting booklet with a local bird on each page. Tick off or name the birds you see in the school grounds.
- Write an advert for your seed cake, advertising it to bird lovers. You could even sell some at your school fête to raise funds.
- Research more about your local birds. Find out whether the baby birds look different to the adult birds.
- Design a seed cake style food for the animal that hatched out of your odd egg. Write the recipe for how to make your fantasy seed cake. Explain how each ingredient is important for its health.
- Role-play being a bird expert. Explain how to recognise different bird species and how to look after them.

Look out for evidence of scientific thinking and learning

- The children show interest in learning about the local bird species.
- The children can identify local bird species.
- The children ask questions, e.g. do all birds eat seeds?

———————————————

9 *Pirates Love Underpants*

Claire Freedman and Ben Cort (2012)

TOPIC PLANNER

Story link	Science: Science skills	Activity	Page
Underpants	Observing closely Devising a simple test Using simple features to sort and group	Sorting underpants (investigation)	166–7
Pirate maps	Simple tests and spotting patterns	Which paper rolls best? Rolling paper maps around dowel (investigation)	171–2
Moving pirate ships	Ask simple question and answer in different ways	How many ways can you move a ship? (activity)	174–5
Following footprints	Observing and identifying	Who made the footprints? Making footprints in sand Set out footprint paint trap (activity)	178–9
The rickety bridge	Simple tests using simple equipment Gathering and recording data	Which is the strongest bridge? (investigation)	183–4
Into the cave!	Observing, simple test and sorting materials	Which material makes the darkest shadows? (investigation)	188
Shhh – they're sleeping!	Observing and comparing (measuring and recording simple data)	Design an intruder alarm! Which is the quietest surface to walk on? (activity)	191–2
I Spy Pirates!	Observing closely	Making water lenses (extension activity 6+)	194–5

Story link	Science:	Activity	Page
Keep your underpants up!	Observing Measuring and recording simple data To answer simple question	Which is the stretchiest elastic? (investigation)	198

This chapter is designed to give you lots of different investigations that will allow you to improve and assess the children's science skills. So, look out for the extra 'Science Skills' that will flag up which skills to focus on as you observe the class, listen to their reasoning and look at their work.

UNDERPANTS

Story link

The pirates all have different underpants. And they love them!

THE SCIENCE: The different properties of materials

We use lots of different materials in our daily lives. We tend to choose the best material for the job in hand by considering the properties of that material: materials that don't let the water through are good for raincoats but useless for straining jam!

The properties you encounter in this activity will depend on the materials you have to hand. I suggest you look for the following types of material to give the children the widest selection of properties to test:

- waterproof
- absorbent
- transparent (see-through)
- opaque (you can't see through it)
- reflective/shiny

- matt/not shiny
- strong (will not snap easily)
- weak (will snap or tear)
- tough (not easily abraded)
- delicate (easily abraded)

Absorbent/waterproof: when a material absorbs water, the water moves into the tiny spaces in the material. This occurs by capillary action. For an explanation of water moving up through paper using capillary action see *The Tiny Seed* chapter (p. 111). Waterproof materials have often been treated with something such as rubber, plastic or wax. Water cannot pass through these materials. Pirates might prefer waterproof underpants or absorbent ones – you can decide which is more useful!

Transparent/transparent/opaque: when light passes through a material, we can see through it, and it is said to be transparent. As a rule of thumb, you can see detail through transparent materials, such as the print in a book. You can see light but no detail through a translucent material. Shower curtains are often translucent. When the light is blocked by a material, we can't see through it, and it is said to be opaque. Wood, metal and felt are opaque. Many fibres used in materials are opaque but if they are loosely woven you may be able to see through the holes. Pirates want their underpants to be opaque!

Reflective/matt: light reflects off shiny surfaces so we see the light (or an image) on the shiny surface. Baubles, foil and water are all reflective surfaces. Some materials are made to be especially reflective so they can help cars to see us in the dark by reflecting back the light from the headlights. When a material is not reflective (matt), some (or all) of the light is absorbed by the material. Pirates might like to have underpants that absorb light so they are not seen when they are creeping up on other pirates.

Strong (not easily snapped): in general, strong materials are made from strong, tightly packed fibres. Pirates would want their underpants to be strong.

Tough (not easily abraded): for the science of different fibres see the chapter *Traction Man Is Here* (p. 56). Pirates would want their pants to be made from tough fibres!

What do the children need to know?

- Different materials have different properties.
- These properties have particular names (see above) and one material can have many properties.

 INVESTIGATION: Sorting underpants

You will need:

- pictures of colourful underpants, like the ones on the flyleaf of the book. You'll need enough for the whole group to work with and there should be different shapes, colours and patterns
- a variety of different materials, e.g. PVC coated tablecloth, thin cotton, denim, netting, foil, paper, greaseproof paper, fleece, kitchen towel, clear plastic, linen, sack cloth, shiny fabrics, tissue paper etc. Aim to have lots of bright patterns so they are like the underpants.

Cut the materials into underpants shapes for extra authenticity

- a piratical looking treasure chest or suitcase
- torches
- trays
- weights
- pots of water
- brillo pads/scrubbing brushes
- bags
- pipettes

Storify the science

Read the story from start to finish. Then return to the flyleaf and admire all the different pants. Pick two and try to find something that is the same and something that is different about the underpants.

Give out the pictures of underpants and ask the children to sort them into groups. Ask the children to give each group a name. Listen to their ideas. They may come up with groups that are based on a variety of different properties, e.g. red ones (colour), stripy ones (pattern) and long ones (size/shape). Write down all the words they use and try to categorise them into colours, patterns and size/shape. They may include the type of fabric. Now ask them to only use one category – sort them into different colours or different patterns. Swap pictures and try sorting again. Keep sorting until you can see they are able to sort into groups using one criterion, e.g. red vs not red or spotty vs not spotty. For more details see *The Tiny Seed* chapter (pp. 93–5).

Return to the book and ask the children what would happen if one of the pirates got their underpants wet in the sea. Dip one of the paper pictures of underpants into water. Note how it collapses and falls apart. Look distressed and seek the children's advice as the pirates spend large amounts of time on the water and their favourite underpants could get wet and fall apart like this. Let the children tell you that real underpants are not made from paper and they can go in the washing machine and not fall apart.

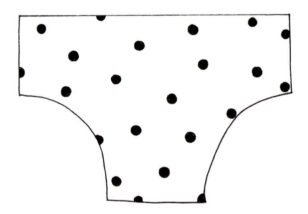

Ask the children about underpants and what they are made from and discuss why it is a good idea not to make them from paper (as they need washing).

Show them the suitcase/treasure chest. Dramatically pull out a pair of underpants (small under-pants shaped piece of fabric) and ask the children why it might be a pirate's favourite. Discuss why we like certain clothes, e.g. soft, doesn't wear out, dries quickly, etc. They might suggest their favourites have a nice pattern. Encourage the children to think of practical reasons rather than aesthetics.

 ## Set the challenge

You are going to investigate the properties of these underpants. You will then be able to suggest which underpants would keep a pirate bottom dry on a rainy day, which underpants would show up best if they fell off the ship in the dark, which underpants would wear out the slowest or dry the fastest on washing day.

First, look closely at all the pants. Use your hands, your eyes and even a magnifying glass.

Next, decide how you might want to sort the underpants. For example, you might want to sort the pants into 'waterproof' and 'not waterproof'. Or you might want to sort the underpants into 'shiny' and 'not shiny'.

Now, decide how you will test the underpants to decide which group they go into.

Test your underpants and sort them into two groups.

Now you can recommend a group of underpants that would be good for a particular purpose, e.g. This is the group of underpants that would keep you dry in the rain.

 # Teacher's top tips

The important skills here are observation, devising a simple test and sorting into groups according to the results.

Encourage the children to think about how to carry out their own simple test. Try to facilitate their ideas if you can, even the ones that won't work.

You may need to show them ways to test the underpants to get them started. Here are some ideas:

Waterproof vs absorbent	Drip 10 drops of water from a pipette onto the underpants. Does the water sink in?
Transparent vs opaque	Can you read text through the underpants?
Reflective vs matt	Do the underpants sparkle when you shine a torch at them?
Weak vs strong	Can I hold a heavy weight in the underpants?
Tough vs delicate	Is the material scuffed if I scrub ten times with a brillo pad?

Depending on the age and ability of your children, you may want to provide a way to record their sorting or you may choose to do the entire activity in groups and listen to their ideas or ask them to put the underpants into hoops according to their properties. A record sheet might look like this:

Material	Do the underpants reflect light? Yes/No	Group of underpants that reflect light	Group of underpants that don't reflect light
A	yes		
B	yes		
C	no	A B D	C E
D	yes		
E	no		

At the end of the session, have a big discussion about all the different ways the underpants were sorted and all the different features that were observed or tested.

KEY QUESTIONS to help children to move towards an understanding:

- What do you want to try?
- Why did you choose that?
- Can you find some things that are . . .?
- Do all the materials do that?
- Are they the same in some way?
- What do you think will happen?

Science skills

Remember to look out for evidence of **observing closely or devising a simple test and using simple features to sort and group**.

Watch to see whether the children spend time using a hand lens, their eyes and their hands to explore and compare all the fabrics.

They may come up with their own idea for a simple test to compare the properties of each material. Look for evidence of the test being applied to all the materials in the same way.

They may group the materials many times in the sessions, according to different features. Listen out for them making decisions about how to group the materials that are based on their features.

 ## What next?

If you want to record your findings in a creative way then you could:

- Ages 4–5: choose three pairs of underpants, stick them into a results table (like the one below) and show your results by ticking or writing yes/no to answer the question.

Underpants (put underpants in this column)	Waterproof?

- Create washing lines of groups of underpants that you sorted.
- Draw a piratical cupboard with two or three compartments. Write a label on each compartment to show what property the contents of each compartment has. Draw or stick the right pants in each compartment.

- Write an advert for a pair of underpants, describing each property and how it could be useful.
- Write a story about a pirate who gets into trouble and his underpants turn out to be very handy, e.g. he falls overboard and his sparkly underpants reflect the moonlight so he can be found by his shipmates or she gets caught in the rain but her waterproof underpants keep the treasure map dry.

Look out for evidence of scientific thinking and learning

- The children engage in testing the materials.
- The children find their own way to test the materials and review whether their method works.
- The children make observations, e.g. these underpants are all really stretchy.
- The children make links, e.g. these underpants are made from glittery material so they will all sparkle when I shine the torch on them.
- The children ask questions, e.g. will these underpants leak in the rain?
- The children test ideas to find answers, e.g. if I drip water on the underpants I can see whether the water will go through.
- The children can sort the materials into groups according to their properties, e.g. these are all waterproof.

PIRATE MAPS

Story link
The pirates unfurl the map.

THE SCIENCE: Paper thickness

Different papers and cards come in different thicknesses and have different numbers of fibres pressed together in different ways.

Thin papers will roll smoothly and fold with a clean, straight fold. Thicker papers are harder to roll and fold without the structure cracking.

What do the children need to know?

- Different papers have different properties so we use them for different purposes.

INVESTIGATION: Which paper rolls best?

You will need:

- strips of different papers and card (about 10 cm long and 2 cm wide), e.g. tissue, kitchen towel, newspaper, photocopier paper, sugar paper, thin card, thick card, cereal boxes, stiff cardboard
- corrugated card cut into strips (10 × 2 cm) along the grain (won't roll smoothly)
- corrugated card cut into strips (10 × 2 cm) across the grain (will flatten and roll fairly smoothly)
- dowel, rolling pins or glue sticks with a round barrel about 2 cm in diameter.
- a ready-made pirate map made out of thick brown card that crumples and rips as it is rolled and tends to roll back up when you try to read it.

 # Storify the science

Return to the book and look at the page where the pirates are looking at the map.

Show the children your thick card treasure map. Deliberately struggle with the map and fail to flatten it back out – let it roll up. Get cross with the map and show how the pictures are ripped where the card folds. Tell them you really wanted to make maps with them but it's just not working. Let the children give you advice and suggest other types of paper you could use instead. Ask them how you could find the best paper or card for making maps.

 # Set the challenge

You are going to investigate which paper or card rolls up smoothly.

Before you start, think about how you will make sure that you roll all the paper/card in the same way.

After you have rolled the paper/card, check the paper/card for creases that will weaken the paper and make it hard to read.

Which paper do you think would be best to use for making treasure maps?

Is there a pattern in your results?

 # Teacher's top tips

The important skills here are carrying out a simple test and finding a pattern. The children should find that the thicker paper/card creases more than the thinner paper. It will also be related to the rigidity of the paper/card – the more rigid the paper/card, the more it will crack and crease.

KEY QUESTIONS to help children to move towards an understanding:

- What do you want to try?
- Why did you choose that?
- Can you find some things that are . . .?
- Do all the materials do that?
- Are they the same in some way?
- Can you see a pattern?

Science skills

Remember to look out for evidence of **spotting a pattern**.

The test design will be set by the fact that the paper/card is pre-cut into strips to make the test as fair as possible. Providing dowel or glue-sticks for them to roll the paper/card around removes the opportunity for the children to try different sizes of roll. However, in this activity, you are offering the children a chance to spot a pattern so keeping the test design the same for all will help that pattern to emerge, so it is worth restricting the testing method in this case.

 # What next?

If you want to record your findings in a creative way then you could:

- Ages 4–5: make a treasure map and write the name of the type of paper you chose on the map.
- Choose the paper you think would make the best treasure map. Draw your own map and roll it up.
- Collect up all the paper strips you rolled and write a word to describe what the paper looks like after rolling, on each paper. Stick them onto a sheet of flat paper and write a sentence about what you found out.
- Role-play being a map maker explaining to a pirate about rolling paper. Suggest which paper would make the best map to the pirate.

 # Look out for evidence of scientific thinking and learning

- The children make observations, e.g. this paper is very floppy.
- The children make links, e.g. all the floppy papers roll smoothly.
- The children test ideas to find answers, e.g. I'm going to try rolling these three pieces of card to see which gets most creased.
- The children can identify a pattern – the thicker the paper the harder it is to roll smoothly.

———————————————

MOVING PIRATE SHIPS

Story link
The ship sails.

THE SCIENCE: Forces

This set of activities involves making a land ship on wheels! It could all be done with floating ships but you'd need a large body of ankle deep water as well so I've opted for land ships that will work on any shiny floor.

There are lots of ways to make something move. They all involve a force because nothing will start to move unless a force is applied to it.

If you move a ship using wind then the wind is pushing it.

If you move a ship (on wheels) by sliding it down a slope then gravity is pulling it down.

If you attach a balloon to the ship (on wheels) then the jet of air causes thrust that moves the ship forwards. Air is forced out of the balloon by the sides of the balloon pushing on it. This creates a jet of air pushing backward out of the balloon. Newton's Third Law states that for every action there is an equal and opposite reaction so if you push air out backwards it will also push the car forwards. Imagine sitting on a wheelie chair facing a wall. You push out forwards with your legs on the wall but the chair moves backwards. It works in the same way.

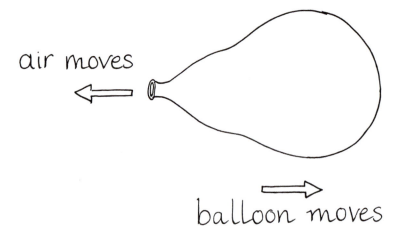

air moves

balloon moves

What do the children need to know?

• There are lots of ways to move a ship – you can use a push, a pull or gravity.

ACTIVITY: How many ways can you move a ship?

You will need:

- small rectangles of card (15 cm × 10 cm)
- straws
- thin dowel or kebab sticks (with pointy end removed)
- card wheels with centre hole to fit dowel/kebab stick
- tape
- cotton reels or cubes of foam packaging
- thin paper for sails
- glue gun (adults only)
- balloons
- an electric fan (supervised by an adult)
- newspapers for wafting
- ramps.

 ## Storify the science

Return to the page where the pirates are sailing away. Explain that you are going to make some ships that sail on land.

Show the children how to tape the straws to the base of the card and thread the dowel/kebab stick through the straws and fix wheels to the dowel/kebab stick so that the ship base will roll freely.

Now you are ready to glue gun the cotton reels or foam onto the base (adults only). There are lots of possible designs so you may want to find one that suits the equipment you have by looking online. The aim of this part of the process is to stand a sail upright on the base. Make sure the sail is well anchored so it can catch the wind. (See next page.)

 ## Set the challenge

You are going to find as many ways as you can to move your ship.

You can use the equipment your teacher has provided. You can even add things to your ship to make it move.

As you move your ship, think about what is making it move.

See how many different ways you can find to move your ship.

Teacher's top tips

The important skills here are finding lots of different ways to fulfil the challenge so try to keep the children thinking until they have found a variety of ways.

You might begin by asking the children to move their ships in different ways. Then move on to asking specific questions to make them think more deeply:

Can you make it move without touching it?

Can you make it move quickly?

Can you make it move very slowly?

Can you keep it moving at a steady speed?

You could even have a race if your children enjoy a bit of competition.

This is best done in a large space with a smooth floor such as the hall. Make sure there is equipment such as ramps, fans and newspapers for wafting available for children to use, without telling them how to use it.

If you can, leave a space available for children to continue with this activity at their own pace.

KEY QUESTIONS to help children to move towards an understanding:

- What do you want to try?
- Why did you choose that?
- Try that again. Did the same thing happen?
- Why do you think that happens?
- How could you make it faster?

Science skills

Remember to look out for evidence of **finding different ways to answer the question**.

Take time to talk to the children and listen to the way they describe moving the ship. If they seem to be stuck using one way, encourage them to try something new. You can stop the session and allow children to demonstrate their ideas to one another which will inspire new ideas in the other children.

 # What next?

If you want to record your findings in a creative way then you could:

- Ages 4–5: make a mini Ship's Log Book. On each page draw a way in which you moved your ship and label it, e.g. push, blow or fan.
- Draw all the ways you made your ship move and annotate the drawings to explain how you moved it.

- Video your ship moving. Write a voice-over to explain how you made it move each time.
- Make up an adventure tale for a tiny pirate that lives on your boat. Include all of the ways you moved your boat in the adventure.

Look out for evidence of scientific thinking and learning

- The children find new ways to move their ship.
- The children make observations, e.g. the fan can only blow it a little way.
- The children make links, e.g. it rolls downhill like I do on my bike.
- The children ask questions, e.g. does it go faster if I fan with the paper wide open or folded up?
- The children test ideas to find answers, e.g. can I move it faster with a newspaper fan than the electric fan can?
- The children check their strategies for moving the ship and change them if they are not working.
- The children review their different ways of moving the ship and can tell you which was easiest or which moved the ship the fastest or furthest.

FOLLOWING FOOTPRINTS

Story link
The pirates follow the footprints.

 THE SCIENCE: Footprints

Prints in the sand will be the same shape as the object that made them.

The depth of the footprint will vary according to the force with which it was made. Heavy people or people jumping into the sand will make deeper footprints than their lighter, gentler counterparts.

What do the children need to know?

- You can identify the person or animal from the shape of the footprint as different animals have different shaped feet.
- You can make different prints by jumping or tip-toeing.

ACTIVITY: Who made the footprints?

You will need:

- large sand trays at floor level or a sand pit

- damp sand

- a rake to smooth it over

- rulers

- poster paint (non-toxic)

- paper

- a footprint tunnel (can be homemade)

- peanut butter or dog food (avoid nuts if your children have allergies)

- tent pegs.

 ## Storify the science

If you have a sandpit, start there! If not, set up a tray of sand, as big as possible, in your class-room area.

Before the lesson, smooth over the sand to make it flat. (It works best if the sand is slightly damp.) If possible, allow the children to see the flat sand and admire how tidy it looks and ask them not to tread it in as you're preparing something. Then, while they are out at play, ask a member of staff to come and put a footprint in the sand. The shoe should be distinctive in some way (by the tread or shape or size) and definitely bigger than the children's shoes.

When the children come in, let them notice the footprint or show it to them, looking shocked and upset. Without upsetting the children, accuse them of treading in your sandpit and tell them you have no idea who it was but you'd like to find out. When they realise that the shoe is way too big they may helpfully start accusing the other adults in the room and you can start the process of working out whose shoe it might be. Take a photo of the print in case it gets spoiled and start looking for the culprit.

To find the culprit, have a look at the shoe and match up the size and the tread and the shape with the sole. Once you've found them, return to the book.

Turn to the page where the pirates follow the footprints. Notice that there is only one set of prints. Turn to the page of sleeping pirates. Look for the one who made the footprints. All of the sleeping pirates are wearing boots! Who could have made the prints? They may suggest the monkey (who is not wearing boots) or the dog. But it is impossible to tell without looking at the soles of their feet.

Set the challenge

You are going to see what kind of footprints your feet make. You can go barefoot if your teacher says it's safe.

Try these things:

- walking
- jumping
- hopping
- tip-toeing
- running (if your sandpit is big enough).

Look at the footprints you made. Are they all the same? What is different about them? Look closely with your eyes. Measure the prints if you like.

You could set a challenge for a friend. Ask them to close their eyes. Now make footprints with your feet and when your friend opens their eyes, see if they can tell how you made them. Were you jumping or walking?

 ## Finale

At this point, you may like to make footprints or handprints with paint and paper. Look at the prints. Ask the children if they can tell what made the prints?

Show them the footprint tunnel. (This is a sturdy triangular prism shape in durable card or plastic, open at both ends and large enough for small mammals to walk thorough. You can find full instructions on the internet.) Show the children how to prime the tunnel with a food source (peanut butter, being aware of children with allergies, or dog food), non-toxic paint and clean paper. Explain how animals visiting the school grounds at night might come into the tunnel to find the food and leave their footprints behind.

Choose a place where small mammals might go – along field boundaries or hedgerows, for example, and peg down the tunnel and leave it overnight.

In the morning, retrieve the paper inside the tunnel and use a mammal footprint identification guide (loads on the internet) to identify any mammals visiting your area at night.

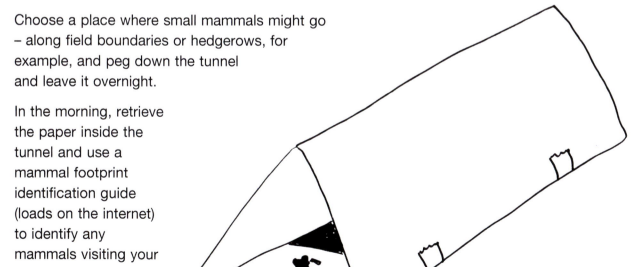

Teacher's top tips

The important skill here is careful observation. Encourage your children to look closely and to measure the footprints. This could be done very informally, e.g. the footprint is as deep as the first joint of my thumb and it is as long as this stick.

KEY QUESTIONS to help children to move towards an understanding:

- What can you see?
- Do they all look the same?
- Can you find one that is different?
- What makes it different?
- Are they the same in some way?

You may want to experiment with the footprint tunnel in advance to find a good spot and a successful food source that attracts the animals you have in your area. Do check the advice of wildlife groups on the internet as they can recommend the right food for particular animals.

Don't leave it anywhere where children with allergies could come across it unsupervised.

Science skills

Remember to look out for evidence of **observing carefully**.

Take time to talk to the children and listen to the way they describe and discuss the footprints. Encourage comparisons and measurements. Listen out for comparative terms such as bigger, deeper, wider.

 ## What next?

If you want to record your findings in a creative way then you could:

- Ages 4–5: create a footprint dance. Use all kinds of ways to move. Think about which part of you is touching the floor. Dance in the sandpit and look at the different footprints you made.
- Make a poster of different animal footprints that you found in the tunnel. Write describing words or the name of the animal next to each print.
- Make a snakes and ladders style game. Start at the pirate ship and end at the treasure. Draw footprints made by the animals who visited your footprint tunnel, on some squares of the board. Animal footprints lead you up the ladder but if you land on a pirate footprint, slide down a snake.
- Measure your handprint and footprint. Ask more questions such as 'Do the children with bigger hands have bigger feet too?'. Now find ways to answer your questions.
- Role-play being an animal expert and tell the class about the animals that visited the school overnight and left their footprints in the tunnel. Explain how you know which animals visited;

- Role-play being pirates who find a footprint left by a robber who stole their gold. How do they work out who the robber was? How do they find the robber? Write the story!

Look out for evidence of scientific thinking and learning

- The children make observations, e.g. this one is deeper.
- The children make links, e.g. all the adults make deeper prints.
- The children ask questions, e.g. which animals have three toes?
- The children test ideas to find answers, e.g. I think I'll make a really deep print if I jump really hard.

THE RICKETY BRIDGE

Story link

The pirates cross over a rope bridge.

THE SCIENCE: Bridges

The science behind bridge design is pretty complex but there are basic ideas that the children can access:

Bridges must span a gap. There are various ways to solve the problem of the bridge sagging in the middle or breaking:

1   anchor the beam to the banks so even if it bends, it won't fall right into the gap;

2   create a really strong beam so it won't bend or sag. This can be done by making it really thick and sturdy, or braced with trusses so it can't bend;

3   put supports under the beam to stop it sagging. These could be columns or arches;

4   support the beam from above by suspending it with cables.

(See next page.)

What do the children need to know?

The beam must not be bendy and might need supports to stop it bending under the weight of the pirates.

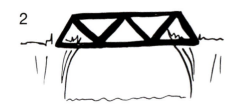

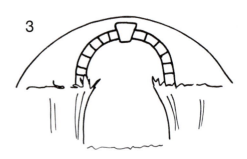

 INVESTIGATION: Which is the strongest bridge?

You will need:

- soft weights, e.g. beanbags or bags of rice (equal in weight)
- Tray 1 containing different types of paper, paper straws, card, cardboard boxes, egg boxes (be aware of allergies) and tape
- Tray 2 containing different yoghurt pots, plastic straws, sheets of plastic and tape
- Tray 3 containing plastic modelling blocks, wooden blocks, construction kit items.

 Storify the science

Look closely at the page where the pirates are crossing the bridge. There are crocodiles below. Ask the children how they might cross the bridge if they were the pirates. Listen to their ideas. Discuss observations such as: it doesn't look strong; they could cross one by one so there is less weight on the bridge; it doesn't fall down because it is pinned onto the cliff edges with stakes; it might be made of cloth or wood but it bends in the middle as there is nothing to hold it up.

Ask them to think about ways to make a stronger bridge. With older children, you might give them a chance to discuss and draw ideas in their groups.

Put two boxes, 20 cm apart, on a table or the floor where they can all see. Show them a bridge you have made from plastic modelling bricks and use it to span the gap. You could even draw crocodiles in the water below the gap. Use short bricks with many joins and little reinforcement so that it is very weak. Lower a beanbag onto the bridge (to represent the pirate) and watch it collapse as you let go of the weight. Point out how disastrous this would be for the pirates!

With younger children, who need experience of working with modelling bricks, spend time making bridges like this one before moving on and spread the activity over several sessions if your children will get more out of it that way.

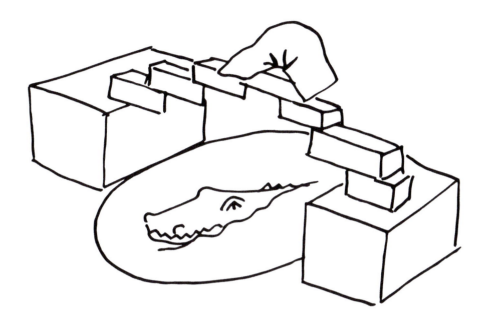

With older children, move on to the challenge. Set up the two boxes as before with about 20 cm between them over the crocodiles or push two tables 20 cm apart to make a gap. You can always increase the gap if it proves too easy!

 # Set the challenge

You are going to investigate bridges for the pirates so they can get across without falling into the crocodile pit.

Your group must make three bridges from three different materials and then test your bridges to see how much weight they can carry to find the strongest bridge.

- Bridge 1 – use paper and card from Tray 1
- Bridge 2 – use plastic pots and straws from Tray 2
- Bridge 3 – use modelling bricks or wooden blocks from Tray 3.

Use materials from one tray only to make each bridge. Before you start, think about:

- the shape of your bridge
- the materials you will need
- how much of each material you should use
- how you will make it strong.

You will have to test each bridge to see how strong it is. Balance a beanbag on the bridge or hang it underneath. See if your bridge is strong enough to hold the weight.

If you think your bridge is really strong, try adding extra beanbags to see how many it will hold. Add them one at a time so you can count them. Write down how much weight each bridge could support.

Which bridge was the strongest?

Why do you think it was the strongest?

Teacher's top tips

The important skills here are testing and collecting some data. Ideally, the children should be able to add weights to the bridge until it collapses, noting which bridge will hold the most.

You could record these results in a pre-drawn table with the following headings:

Materials	Picture of bridge	Weight

This works best if you have a whole afternoon to dedicate to the task. You could split the children into groups and each group builds three different bridges and tests to find the strongest one. If you don't have time to build three bridges per group, build one per group and compare across the class to see whether there are any particular designs that are stronger than others. Make sure at least one bridge is built from each tray.

Allow the children to test out a bridge by putting a weight on it during construction.

Allow time to rebuild and redesign their bridges. If their first attempt collapses easily, encourage them to find the cause of the problem and try to fix it.

With younger children, aim to use weights that won't hurt if dropped on toes. Beanbags are good and you may have a set of matching ones you can use. If not, fill strong kitchen bags with 100 g of cheap rice to create safe 100 g weights.

The items in the trays don't really matter as long as they are different so the children are encouraged to make three different bridges.

KEY QUESTIONS to help children to move towards an understanding:

- What do you want to try?
- Why did you choose that?
- Can you find some things that are . . .?
- Will all the materials do that?
- Are they the same in some way?
- What shape should it be?
- What do you think will happen?

Science skills

Remember to look out for evidence of **testing and collecting data**.

The results can be communicated to you orally as the children tell you what happened. The important things to listen out for are the children making the link between the strength of the bridge and the amount of weight it could hold and being able to offer reasons why one bridge might be stronger than another.

 # What next?

If you want to record your findings in a creative way then you could:

* Ages 4–5: make more bridges between two crates in your outdoor area.
* Take a photo of the strongest bridge. Use sticky notes to annotate the photo to record all the materials you used.
* Role-play being bridge engineers. Inspect all the bridges you made and make notes on your clipboard about what made each bridge strong and what made each bridge weak.
* Design an advert for the strongest bridge. Write captions that highlight the features that make that bridge stronger than the others.
* Role-play being pirates who have to cross one of the bridges. Explain to each other why you would choose to cross one bridge rather than another. Write what you said in speech bubbles to record the conversation.
* Write an entry in the Ship's Log about the day the bridge collapsed. Describe the way you built a strong bridge to replace it.

 # Look out for evidence of scientific thinking and learning

* The children find their own way to make a bridge.
* The children make observations, e.g. the paper is too bendy to hold up the beanbag.
* The children make links, e.g. the paper straws were quite strong so I think the plastic straws will be strong too.
* The children ask questions, e.g. is the card stronger than the paper?
* The children test ideas to find answers, e.g. does it keep it straight if I tape the edges to the banks?
* The children test their bridges and can say which is the strongest one.

_____

INTO THE CAVE!

Story link

The pirates went through the cave

THE SCIENCE: Transparent and opaque

Shadows are formed when light cannot pass through an object. The light is blocked by the object and an area of shadow is produced in the same shape as the object that is blocking the light.

Opaque materials block all the light and create dark shadows.

Light can pass through transparent materials so they make pale shadows.

(There is more information about transparent materials on p. 167 at the beginning of this chapter.)

What do the children need to know?

• Different materials make different shadows.

• You need an opaque material to make a shadow puppet that casts a dark shadow.

INVESTIGATION: Which material makes the darkest shadow?

You will need:

• torches

• a range of different materials including clear plastic, card, cereal boxes with print on them, fabrics with a loose weave, netting, bubblewrap, paper, tissue paper, coloured cellophane wrappers

• white A3 paper

• sheet and pegs and string to make a screen

• strong torch or overhead projector

• kebab sticks (with the pointy end cut off) or lolly sticks to make a support for the shadow puppet.

Storify the science

Before the lesson, set up a large piece of sheet as a screen, with a bright torch behind it – an overhead projector works really well.

Start at the page where the pirates are going through the cave. Note the torch being held up in front of the pirates and their shadows are behind them. If it is a sunny day, take the children outside to look at their own shadows. Note that if the sun is in front of them, their shadow is behind them as their body is blocking out the light.

Return to the book and look at all the animals in the cave – spiders, a snake and the parrot. Ask the children whether they could identify each animal just from the shadow. With your hands behind the screen, hold up a toy snake and a toy spider and then hold up a cardboard cut-out of a parrot. Hold it sideways so that it looks like a straight line. After the children have had a go at guessing the animal, turn the cut-out so that the shape of the parrot is revealed.

Now, put the snake, spider and parrot cut-out where all the children can see them and discuss the differences between the 3D toys and the 2D parrot. Ask them why they think the flat parrot made a very thin shadow. Elicit, that to see the shape of the parrot, you have to hold it 'the right way around'.

Show the children a clear plastic cup or bottle. Ask them what kind of shadow they think it would make. Show them that the shadow is much paler. Ask the children if they think it would make a good shadow puppet. Elicit that you need a dark shadow so you can see the shape of the puppet clearly.

 ## Set the challenge

You are going to find out which materials would make the darkest shadows so you can use them to make a pirate shadow puppet.

Hold your torch so that it shines on the big sheet of white paper. Now try putting different materials in front of the torchlight to see what kind of shadows they make.

Look for the ones that make dark shadows and the ones that make pale shadows.

Sort the materials into groups according to the shadows they make.

Now look at the materials that made dark shadows. Which one of these would you chose to make your shadow puppet? Why?

Now you can make your pirate shadow puppet.

 ## Finale

Create a few simple shapes from modelling bricks. With your hands (and the bricks) hidden behind the screen, show the children the shadow made by the bricks. Invite them to choose bricks from the tray to build the same shape as you have behind the screen. Rotate the shape so they see the different shadows it casts and discuss how hard it is to tell the shape from just the shadow.

Teacher's top tips

The important skills here are observing, carrying out a simple test and sorting the materials into groups.

When you talk about the groups of materials introduce the vocabulary 'opaque' and 'transparent'. Don't worry if the children don't start using them straight away.

Depending on the ability of your children, you could also show them how to cut holes in the puppet to make light spaces or cover holes with coloured cellophane to make coloured parts of the shadow.

Spend time looking at the materials before testing and make predictions about the kind of shadow they might make. Children who have seen the opaque lettering on a cellophane wrapper show up in the shadow may expect the print on an opaque cereal box to show up too. Or they may expect details they draw on the their shadow puppet to show in the shadow.

KEY QUESTIONS to help children to move towards an understanding:

- What do you want to try?
- What do you think you will see?
- Do all the materials do that?
- Are they the same in some way?
- Can you see through it?
- How clearly?
- What can you see using the magnifying glass?
- What is the shadow like?

Science skills

Remember to look out for evidence of **observing, testing and sorting into groups**. Look for evidence that the children can sort the materials according to the shadows they make.

Listen out for them making observations about the materials such as noticing holes in the weave where the light can get through or patches where the transparent materials have opaque lettering on them.

Watch to see whether they are carrying out the test and sorting the materials according to the shadows they make.

What next?

If you want to record your findings in a creative way then you could:

- Ages 4–5: sort all the materials into two boxes – a clear plastic box for materials that make pale shadows and an opaque box for those that make dark shadows. Decide whether you need a third box for materials that make shadows that are neither very dark nor pale.

- Take a photo of your pirate puppet shadow and describe the shadow it makes.

- Write a play for your pirate puppets. Video your play and, at the end, include a section where you explain why you chose the materials you used to make your puppet.

Look out for evidence of scientific thinking and learning

- The children make observations, e.g. the green cellophane makes a green shadow.

- The children make links, e.g. the letters on the card don't show up so the eyes I drew on my puppet won't show up either.

- The children ask questions, e.g. does anything make a blue shadow?

- The children test ideas to find answers, e.g. I'm going to try the blue card to see whether it makes a blue shadow.

- The children can sort the materials into those that make dark shadows and those that don't.

SHH, THEY'RE SLEEPING

Story link
The other pirates are asleep.

THE SCIENCE: Sound

When a hard object is knocked, it vibrates (shakes rapidly). This vibration knocks into air particles around the object and these air particles pass the vibration on to the air particles near them. When this vibration reaches the air particles in our ears, we sense the vibration and thus we hear the sound (see p. 28 for more information).

Different materials vibrate in different ways producing different sounds.

What do the children need to know?

- Different materials make different sounds when you walk on them.

ACTIVITY: Design an intruder alarm!

You will need:

- trays of different objects and materials, e.g. building blocks, stones, sponges, water, foamy water, soft fabric, cardboard boxes, marbles or beads
- data logger or sound meter
- an adult in noisy shoes
- access to outdoor area.

 # Storify the science

Return to the part of the book where the pirates are asleep. Ask the children to be really quiet and listen to sounds in the room. Arrange for one of your other adults to walk around the room in very noisy shoes, e.g. wooden heels on a wooden floor. Notice the sound with the children and discuss other places that are noisy to walk. Lead the class (in groups) on a sound walk around the school. Listen to the sounds their feet make walking over different surfaces. If you have a data logger with a sound meter, or a tablet with an appropriate app, you could measure the noise level of each surface.

Return to the classroom and discuss the noisiest surfaces and the quietest ones.

Now provide some trays of different materials for them to try 'walking' their hands over. You could include building blocks, stones, sponges, water, foamy water, soft fabric, cardboard boxes, marbles or beads. Use whatever you have to hand and fill a tray with each so the children can compare the sounds they make when 'walked on'.

If you have a data logger or sound meter, use it here to measure the different sound levels.

 # Set the challenge

Try walking your hands through the different trays. Which ones are noisy when you walk on them?

You are going to design a garden where the pirates can take a nap and no one will be able to creep up on them without their footsteps being heard. Draw a picture of your design.

Make sure there is a quiet place in the centre of your garden for the pirates' hammocks or beds. Now, decide how you will design the rest of the garden to be noisy underfoot so it acts as an intruder alarm!

Make sure you label each area of the garden to show what you will use as the surface.

Teacher's top tips

The important skill here is observing – using ears and eyes – and comparing the sounds made. You may be able to measure the sound too and thus collect some data.

Put the wet trays on one table to avoid everything getting soaked!

Children will tend to want to hit the trays as hard as possible – encourage the children to 'walk' with their hands not jump!

You could just design your garden on paper or you could use a tray and lay out different materials to make a model of the garden.

Be prepared to try out the ideas that the children may have, if you can find the resources in school. They might suggest something you haven't tested, such as a tray of spoons.

KEY QUESTIONS to help children to move towards an understanding:

- What do you want to try?
- Why did you choose that?
- Can you find some things that are . . .?
- Do all the materials do that?

- Are they the same in some way?
- Why does it sound like that?
- What is happening when you walk your hands on it?

Science skills

Remember to look out for evidence of **observing and comparing**.

To really compare the sounds the children will need to keep checking back, listening to one then the other. Look out for children who are paying close attention in this way.

 # What next?

If you want to record your findings in a creative way then you could:

- Ages 4–5: make a mini garden in a tray. Choose your materials to be quiet where the pirates are sleeping and noisy around the edges.
- Write words to describe the sounds each material made. If they were loud sounds, write the words in large letters. If they were quiet, try to write them in tiny writing.
- Write a brochure to advertise your 'Intruder Alarm Surfaces' to pirates who want to protect their treasure/ship/garden.
- Make a snakes and ladders style game where you have to creep toward the sleeping pirates but if you land on a noisy square you have to go back a few spaces. Use your knowledge of noisy surfaces to choose the noisiest things to draw in the penalty squares.
- Write a poem in the style of *Going on a Bear Hunt* that describes the journey of a pirate going on a treasure hunt and the sounds made by all the different types of terrain he has to go through.

Look out for evidence of scientific thinking and learning

- The children use their senses to explore the materials.
- The children make observations, e.g. these bricks are really loud.
- The children make links, e.g. all the soft things are quiet.
- The children ask questions, e.g. do they make a noise if you shake the tray?
- The children test ideas to find answers, e.g. I think a tray of spoons would be really loud. Can I try spoons?
- The children can sort the materials into noisy and quiet (and in between).
- The children design a garden that would wake the sleeping pirates if intruders approached.

I SPY PIRATES!

Story link
The pirates drop their telescope!

 ### THE SCIENCE: Lenses

We see objects because rays of light reflect off those objects and into our eyes. The light rays enter through the pupil (which is a hole) and land on the layer of light sensitive cells at the back of our eyes, called the retina. When our retina senses this light, it sends messages to the brain and we see the objects. In the dark, we cannot see anything because no light is entering our eyes.

When an object is seen through a lens, the image of the object may appear larger or smaller than the object really is. This happens because the light passing through the lens changes direction and it may spread the light rays out (diverge) or focus them towards a point (converge).

When light passes through a convex lens (one that is fatter in the centre than at the edges, like a magnifying glass) the light rays converge. Our brain assumes that the light is travelling in a straight line from the object, when in fact the direction of the light changes as it passes through the lens. This causes the image of the object that we see to be much larger than the actual object (as long as our eye is close to the lens).

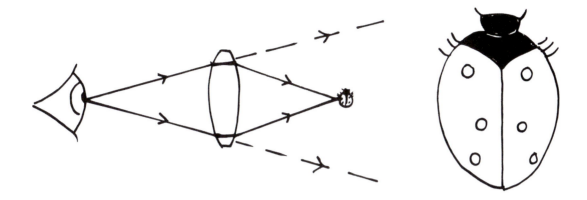

When you drop a water droplet on clear plastic, it will create a dome shape and act like a magnifying glass. This is how scientists first worked out that lenses could be used to magnify images.

What do the children need to know?

• Magnifying glasses and lenses in telescopes are curved and they make things appear to be much larger than they really are.

 EXTENSION ACTIVITY: Making water lenses (for ages 6+)

You will need:

• lots of lenses – magnifying glasses, reading glasses and any other lenses you can find!
• binoculars or simple working telescope/monocular
• card and cardboard tubes from wrapping paper rolls
• tape
• clear plastic
• pipettes
• pots of water
• pots of clear shampoo/washing up liquid/lemonade/milk
• clear plastic sheets or petri dishes (clean with no scratches)
• text with tiny font or very detailed pictures
• hand towels to dry up spillages.

 Storify the science

Return to the page where the pirates are crossing the bridge. They have dropped their telescope. Ask the children whether they think a pirate really needs a telescope. Ask them what they think a telescope does.

Ask the children whether they think they could make a new telescope for the pirates. Listen to all their suggestions and allow them time to create telescopes as a craft activity. Use transparent film or cellophane sheets for the lenses.

Once you have made some telescopes, show the children a real telescope (there are simple plastic ones available from educational suppliers that aren't too expensive) or a pair of binoculars. Notice that the telescope/binoculars makes things that are far away, look closer – it enlarges the image we see. Notice that the ones we made don't do this and come to the conclusion that something is missing.

Show the children as many lenses as you can lay your hands on! Hand lenses should be available in your school. There may also be pots for catching mini-beasts that have magnifying tops. You could also get some reading glasses that have quite a strong magnifying lens in them – cheap ones from the high street will do. Allow them some time to explore the lenses – looking through them and seeing how the world looks different and laying the lenses onto small fonts or detailed pictures to see the image change. You could also have flat plastic sheets available for comparison.

Ask the children to describe the lenses and elicit that they are not flat like the plastic we used in our telescopes – they are thick and curved and smooth.

 ## Set the challenge

You are going to make a lens!

You will need a flat plastic sheet or petri dish. It must be completely clear and without scratches.

Use a pipette to drop two or three drops of water onto the sheet to make one domed droplet of water.

Now carefully slide your water lens over the page of a book.

What does the writing look like through the water droplet lens?

Would you like to try a different liquid?

What did you observe?

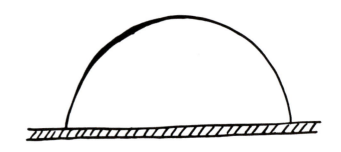

 ## Teacher's top tips

The important skills here are working carefully with equipment and making observations.

If they want to tinker by trying more droplets or less droplets in the water lens then let them try it out.

You could also try making a droplet of other transparent liquids to see whether they will act like magnifiers too. You can buy clear shampoo and washing up liquid. They may like to try lemonade. If they ask to try an opaque liquid – let them try it and allow them to explore their own misconception without leaping in and telling them it won't work.

Clean and dry the plastic before trying something new.

KEY QUESTIONS to help children to move towards an understanding:

- What do you want to try?
- Why did you choose that?
- Do all the liquids do that?
- Are they the same in some way?

- What can you see?
- What else would you like to try?
- What do you think will happen?

Science skills

Remember to look out for evidence of **careful use of equipment and observing**.

It may take a few attempts to be able to create the dome of water using the pipette. They will have to be able to drop one drop of water at a time, which can be a challenge for little hands.

The children may find it hard to move the plastic without disturbing the droplet so look out for evidence that they are taking care to move it steadily.

Look out for evidence that they are observing closely – noting what happens at the edges of the droplet, what happens with different liquids or what shapes the droplet form.

 # What next?

If you want to record your findings in a creative way then you could:

- Draw a tiny picture of a pirate (or use a photocopier to make your picture smaller). Then, explain how to make a water droplet lens to a friend so that they can admire your drawing by using the lens to enlarge the image.

- Write instructions on a computer entitled 'How to make a water droplet lens'. Make the font as small as you can. Show someone the instructions and give them a water droplet lens to enlarge them and make them easier to read!

- Write a story about a pirate who found a tiny map (maybe it was made for fairies or leprechauns) and had to discover how to make a water droplet lens so she could read the map and find the treasure.

 # Look out for evidence of scientific thinking and learning

- The children make observations, e.g. my droplet is a different size to yours.
- The children make links, e.g. the water droplet is curved like my glasses and they both make things bigger.
- The children ask questions, e.g. will it work with washing up liquid?
- The children test ideas to find answers, e.g. I'm going to try using clear washing up liquid to make a lens.
- The children can sort the liquids into those that make good lenses and those that don't.

KEEP YOUR UNDERPANTS UP!

Story link
It's a good idea to check your elastic ...

THE SCIENCE: Elasticity

The word elastic actually refers to a property of materials. Rubber is elastic – it can be stretched and will recoil when released, just like a spring. Consequently, we tend to call rubber bands 'elastic bands'. In this section I will use rubber to describe the material and elastic to describe the property.

Forces can make things move, change speed or stop. They can also change the shape of an object. In order to stretch rubber you have to pull it. This pull force changes its shape.

The greater the pulling force the greater the change in shape . . . until it snaps.

The rubber can stretch because it is made up of large molecules (polymers) that have a tangled and coiled up structure. When you pull the rubber, it pulls the coiled molecules out straighter, within the rubber. When you let go, the molecules coil up again.

Over time, rubber will begin to perish – the air and light will act upon the rubber and make it brittle. It will stop being stretchy and will snap, if pulled, so it is no longer elastic. This is when your underpants are in danger of falling down!

There are many other stretchy materials such as spider silk, muscles fibres, silly putty and lycra. Even metals can be stretched but they may not return to their original shape when released.

What do the children need to know?

- Some materials are elastic.
- Some stretch more than others.

INVESTIGATION: Which is the stretchiest elastic?

You will need:

- a variety of types of elastic materials, e.g. rubber bands, knicker elastic (wide and narrow), elastic cord, clear stretchy plastic thread for beadwork, long hair ties and any other elastic materials you can find. You'll only need a few pieces of each. They should be the same length – 10–20 cm long. You'll find lots of this type of material in a craft shop

- pencils
- rulers
- two pairs of pants (children's)
- weights (250g of rice in a plastic bag)
- a piratical looking treasure chest or suitcase
- lots of different materials – some stretchy that won't recoil – such as thin plastic or bubblewrap, or kitchen roll, some elastic materials that will recoil like balloons and rubber bands, some that don't stretch such as paper.

 ## Storify the science

Before the lesson, set up the strips of elastic material like the diagram below; 10 cm down the elastic materials make a clear mark. If you want to run this activity with a small group then one dowel will be enough. If you want to work with a larger group, you will need more dowels.

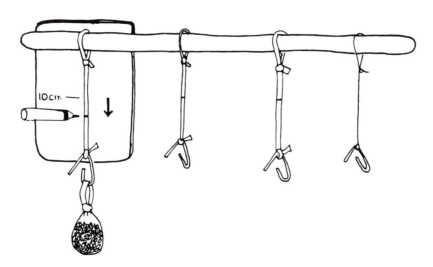

10 cm. →

Later on, these can then be hung between tables and a bag of rice hooked onto the bottom as a weight.

Start at the last page of the book. Read the advice about checking their knicker elastic. Ask the children what happened to the pirates whose knicker elastic was cut.

Return to the treasure chest or suitcase that you used in the first activity in this book. Pull out a couple of pairs of pants (children's might be best for this activity) and ask which they think has the most stretchy elastic. Let the children pull them about and see if they stretch a lot.

Now get out a cheap supermarket plastic bag cut into the shape of knickers. Tell the children that you have noticed that these bags stretch a lot. Pull really hard on the plastic and make it stretch right out. Look really pleased with yourself and tell them this is really stretchy so maybe we could make knickers out of it. Let them tell you that the plastic bag won't ping back into shape so knickers made from that material would just fall off.

Slowly, help the children realise that some materials can be stretched and they will ping back/recoil to their original shape while others will remain stretched. Other materials won't stretch at all.

With younger children you could spend time stretching lots of different materials, from balloons to kitchen towel. The following challenge may be too fiddly so you could just continue to explore the stretchiness of the materials.

With older children, ask what kind of material the pirates should put at the top/the waistband of their underpants to make sure they don't fall down. Elicit that the material should be stretchy and elastic.

Look at the page where the pirates are dancing. All the pirates are different sizes and their knickers are different sizes. For a big pirate to get his knickers up over his tummy, they must be made of something really stretchy.

 # Set the challenge

You are going to find out which elastic material will stretch the most.

Look at the elastic materials on the pole and feel them with your hands. Which one do you think will stretch the most? Why?

Put a mark on the whiteboard level with the mark on the elastic material.

Hang the same weight on each material in turn.

Now put another mark on the white board to show where the bottom of the mark on the elastic material is now. Has it changed? How much has the material stretched? Which one stretches the most?

Use a ruler to measure the gap between the first mark and the second mark. Record your results in a table like this:

Name of material	Amount it has stretched
Rubber band	
Clear plastic cord	

Which one stretched the most?

Teacher's top tips

The important skills here are measuring and recording simple data so the test method can be set in advance as you are not focussing on designing the test.

Encourage correct use of the ruler – you may want to practise this in a related maths lesson beforehand.

Encourage the children to draw their own results table, if they are able. It doesn't have to be neat but encourage them to use the right column headings so that their results are organised.

If you want the children to test the elastic in their own way then that can be done but children under 7 often find it hard to design a test that is fair so the results collected may not be valid.

You may want to look at the equipment with the children and see whether they can work out why you marked the elastic materials at 10 cm and hung the same weight on each.

You may find that the stretchiest material is really not very strong so you may want to discuss which one was stretchy and strong.

KEY QUESTIONS to help children to move towards an understanding:

- What do you want to try?
- Why did you choose that?
- Can you find some things that are . . .?
- Do all the elastic materials do that?
- Are they the same in some way?
- What do you think will happen?

Science skills

Remember to look out for evidence of **careful measuring and recording the results in a table**.

At this level, careful measuring might be looking at the marks and ranking them in order from least stretched to most stretched. It might involve using a ruler to measure the distance between two marks. You'll need to work out where your children are in their understanding and look for evidence that they have measured in a way that is meaningful to them.

Likewise, drawing a table and filling it in might not be meaningful to your children so you may need to look for other evidence of recording of their results and you may need to talk to the children to work out how they have recorded it

What next?

If you want to record your findings in a creative way then you could:

- Ages 4–5: stick a piece of the materials you think are the stretchiest onto a picture of pirate underpants. Decide which one you think is the stretchiest of all and stick a gold star next to it.

- Role-play at being the large pirate captain and the first mate. The pirate captain complains that he can't get his underpants on as the waistband won't stretch far enough. The first mate makes suggestions about which material he could use in the waistband instead.

- Write a report for an underpants factory on your testing. Include your results and make your suggestion about the best kind of elastic materials (i.e. the stretchiest) to use in pirate underpants to accommodate even the largest pirate.

- Design the perfect pair of pirate underpants. Label all the parts and make sure you select the most appropriate material for the waistband.

Look out for evidence of scientific thinking and learning

- The children make observations, e.g. this one is really stretchy.

- The children make links, e.g. the thin ones all stretch more easily.

- The children ask questions, e.g. will it stretch more with more weight?

- The children test ideas to find answers, e.g. I'm going to try adding more weight to see if does stretch more.

- The children can sort the materials according to stretchiness.

———————————————

References

Carle, E. (1970). *The Tiny Seed*. New York: Thomas J. Crowell.

Coates, D., and Wilson, H. (2003). *Challenges in Primary Science: Meeting the Needs of Able Young Scientists at Key Stage 2*. London: NACE/Fulton Publication.

Davies, B. (2016). *The Storm Whale in Winter*. London: Simon & Schuster Children's Books.

Freedman, C., and Cort, B. (2012). *Pirates Love Underpants*. London: Simon & Schuster Children's Books.

Gravett, E. (2008). *The Odd Egg*. London: Macmillan's Children's Books.

Grey, M. (2006). *Traction Man is Here*. London: Red Fox Picture Books.

Johnston, J. (2004). The value of exploration and discovery. *Primary Science Review* (85), 21–3.

Murphy, J. (1980). *Peace at Last*. London: Macmillan Children's Books.

Smith, C., and Pottle, J. (2015). *Science Through Stories*. Stroud, UK: Hawthorn Press.

Stickland, P. S., and Stickland, H. (2014). *Dinosaur Roar*. London: Picture Corgi (Random House Children's Publishers).

Watson, J. (1968). *The Double Helix*. New York: Atheneum Press.

Useful websites

ASE: www.ase.org.uk

Insect Lore: www.insectlore.co.uk

Living Eggs: www.livingeggs.co.uk

RSPB: www.rspb.org.uk

Sarah Bearchell: www.bearchell.co.uk

Storytelling Schools: www.storytellingschools.com

Thinking Doing Talking Science: www.thinkingdoingtalkingscience.org

Index